D0627293

PQ
652
.I8
.Z6

Date Due

AUG 1 6 1974

TWAYNE'S WORLD AUTHORS SERIES

A Survey of the World's Literature

Sylvia E. Bowman, Indiana University

GENERAL EDITOR

SPAIN

Gerald Wade, Vanderbilt University

EDITOR

Tomás de Iriarte

(TWAS 228)

TWAYNE'S WORLD AUTHORS SERIES (TWAS)

The purpose of TWAS is to survey the major writers —novelists, dramatists, historians, poets, philosophers, and critics—of the nations of the world. Among the national literatures covered are those of Australia, Canada, China, Eastern Europe, France, Germany, Greece, India, Italy, Japan, Latin America, the Netherlands, New Zealand, Poland, Russia, Scandinavia, complemented by Twayne's United States Authors Yiddish, and Latin Classical literature. This survey is complemented by Twayne's United State Authors Series and English Authors Series

The intent of each volume in these series is to present a critical-analytical study of the works of the writer; to include biographical and historical material that may be necessary for understanding, appreciation, and critical appraisal of the writer; and to present all material in clear, concise English—but not to vitiate the scholarly content of the work by doing so.

Tomás de Iriarte

By R. MERRITT COX
Duke University

Twayne Publishers, Inc. :: New York

For Myra Lubchansky

Preface

This book is intended to be a general study of the life and work of Tomás de Iriarte. In five chapters, it is to be considered as divided into three general sections: (1) Iriarte's life and, briefly, his works as they affect his life (Chapter 1); (2) specific works studied in detail (Chapters 2–4); (3) criticism of Iriarte (Chapter 5). This final chapter also includes a short concluding section for the entire book. The chronology on the following pages comes from various sources, but basically it relies on a sketch made by Viera y Clavijo before Iriarte's death. Facts are added from Cotarelo and others. The bibliography at the end is selective; only the most pertinent commentaries on Iriarte and his times have been included.

Regarding the presentation of the contents of this book, three remarks may be helpful. Since the work of Iriarte is so varied, it was difficult to set up the divisions for discussing it without being somewhat arbitrary. As a result one or two literary productions have received only passing mention. Such is the case, for example, with the unfinished translation of the *Aeneid* and the eleven *Epistles* Iriarte wrote at various times. These latter, important as a group, nevertheless defy any attempt at classification and are referred to usually as examples for an occasional point at issue. Also it may be necessary at times to repeat certain facts concerning the publication of a work or perhaps the polemics involving Iriarte, and similar matters. This procedure occurs principally because of the outline form of Chapter 1, a form which requires that succeeding chapters merit amplifications of the material found there. It seems advisable also to point out that for many of the quotations from Iriarte only the English form is necessary since the Spaniard's material is readily accessible in its original form. The translations are my own except for those from the *Literary Fables,* for which Devereaux's 1855 translation is used.

It is hoped that certain new ideas will become evident and accepted as the reader goes through the book. However, it should be realized from the beginning that my purpose is more to give a total picture of Iriarte than simply to emphasize new viewpoints I myself may have. I hope that with this purpose in mind students of Spanish literature—at any level—will find here a concise, precise history of Iriarte and that they will get from this total picture the individual facts needed for any comprehension of the fabulist and the period in which he lived.

R. Merritt Cox

Durham
February, 1971

Contents

Chronology

1750 September 18: Tomás de Iriarte is born in Puerto de la Cruz on Tenerife (Canary Islands) to Bernardo de Iriarte and Bárbara de las Nieves de Oropesa.

1760 Formal Latin instruction begins for Tomás in La Orotava under his brother Juan Tomás de Iriarte.

1764 Iriarte writes some Latin verses upon leaving the Canary Islands to go to Madrid and live with his uncle Juan de Iriarte, librarian to the king and a renowned authority in Latin and the Humanities. The profound influence of the uncle on the intellectual development of Tomás begins in this year.

1769– Iriarte translates many plays to be presented at the various
1772 royal palaces in Spain. Among them are *El filósofo casado* (*The Married Philosopher*) and *El huérfano de la China* (*The Chinese Orphan*).

1770 A play begun by Iriarte a year or two earlier and called *Hacer que hacemos (The Busybody)* appears under the anagram of Tirso Imareta. In this year Nicolás Fernández de Moratín's play *Hormesinda* is presented marking the beginning of the open clash in the field of drama between the Neoclassicists and the Traditionalists. Iriarte's defense of the Neoclassicists (although not too warmly of Moratín's play) is called *Carta escrita al Pardo por un caballero de Madrid a un amigo suyo (Letter Written by a Gentleman of Madrid to His Friend)*.

1771 At the death of his uncle Iriarte succeeds him as Official Translator of the First Secretariat of State. The *Gramática latina (Latin Grammar)* of Juan de Iriarte is printed posthumously under the correction and supervision of his nephew. In this year Iriarte writes a poem in both Latin and Spanish celebrating the birth of the Prince, Charles

III's grandson, and the instituting of the Order of Charles III.

1772 Iriarte is given the directorship of the gazette *El mercurio histórico y político (The Historical and Political Mercury)*.

1773 *Los literatos en cuaresma (Writers in Lent)* appears. Iriarte begins a very incisive correspondence with Cadalso concerning events in the capital while Cadalso is elsewhere in the country.

1776 Iriarte is named Archivist of the Supreme Council of War.

1777 Iriarte's translation of Horace's *Poetics* appears. In the same year he writes a *Carta familiar y apologética (Familiar and Apologetic Letter)* in defense of his translation.

1778 The translation is criticized by Juan José López de Sedano, the editor of the *Parnaso español (Spanish Parnassus)*. Iriarte responds with a polemical dialogue *Donde las dan las toman (Give and Take)*.

1779 Iriarte enters his eclogue *La felicidad de la vida del campo (The Happiness of Country Life)* in the Royal Academy's literary competition for 1779. It is printed in 1780.

1780 At the beginning of this year appears Iriarte's poem *La música (Music)*. Several other minor works are also written: *Plan de una Academia de Ciencias y Bellas Letras (Plan For an Academy of Sciences and Letters), Reflexiones sueltas (Miscellaneous Reflections)*, and *Consideraciones que se han tenido presentes para la extensión del plan de la Academia de Ciencias y Buenas [sic] Letras (Considerations For the Extension of the Plan)*.

1781 *Reflexiones sobre la égloga de Batilo (Reflections Concerning the Eclogue Batilo)* appears, it being Iriarte's polemical work on the awarding of the 1779 Academy prize to Meléndez Valdés. It is answered by Juan Pablo Forner in *Cotejo de las églogas que ha premiado la Real Academia de la Lengua (Comparison of the Eclogues Awarded Prizes by the Royal Academy of the Language)*. The bitter polemic between these two enemies thus begins.

1782 Iriarte's most famous work, the *Fábulas literarias (Literary Fables)*, is published. The collection is immediately criticized by Forner in his *El asno erudito (The Erudite Ass)*. Iriarte responds in kind with his *Para casos tales suelen tener los maestros oficiales (For Just Such Cases Do They*

Have Trained Teachers). In this same year Félix María de Samaniego writes an attack on the *Fables* and on Iriarte: *Observaciones sobre las Fábulas literarias originales de D. Tomás de Iriarte (Observations Concerning the "Original" Literary Fables of Tomás de Iriarte).* Forner continues the polemic with *Los gramáticos: historia chinesca (The Grammarians: A Chinese History).*

1786   *Carta al R. P. Fr. Francisco de los Arcos (Letter to the Most Reverend Francisco de los Arcos)* is composed to mock the attitude of the rather ingenuous writer named in the title. The Inquisition begins its suit against Iriarte.

1787   The first edition of Iriarte's complete works, in six volumes, is made.

1788   *El señorito mimado (The Pampered Youth)* is produced. *La señorita mal-criada (The Ill-Bred Miss)* is published but is not staged until 1791.

1789   Iriarte writes two works directed at the enlightening of youth. One is a translation of Campe's *El nuevo Robinson (The New Robinson).* The other is *(Lecciones instructivas (Instructive Lessons),* not published until 1791.

1790   While in Andalusia, Iriarte writes two plays: *El don de gentes (Winning Ways)* and *Donde menos se piensa salta la liebre (It Would Happen Where Least Expected).* Also the melologue *Guzmán el bueno (Guzmán, The Good),* produced in February, 1791, dates from this trip to the South.

1791   September 17: Iriarte dies, only one day before he would have been forty-one years of age.

1805   The most complete edition of Iriarte's works, in eight volumes, is published.

CHAPTER 1

Life of Tomás de Iriarte

I Background of the Family

OFFICIAL Translator of the First Secretariat of State, General Archivist of the Supreme Council of War, native of Puerto [de la Cruz] de La Orotava de Tenerife . . . his creative faculty, his fertile inspiration, and his well-known talents have made him famous within a very few years both in and outside Spain through his poetic works, his taste in and knowledge of music, his knowledge of different languages, his criticism, and his literary productions. To write a simple catalog of his works is merely to praise him without flattery. . . ." [1] It is with this concise, laudatory paragraph that José de Viera y Clavijo begins his brief study of his contemporary, Tomás de Iriarte. For two reasons this selection is of interest. It shows the regard in which Iriarte was held in 1783 (the date of the first publication of Viera's book). In addition, its statements are made in such fashion as to imply there could be no doubt in anyone's mind of their truth: that is, in his own time it was felt that Iriarte had gained a secure niche in the esteem of his countrymen, a position from which he could not, and should not, be dislodged. The respect which Viera feels is all the more intriguing when one considers that by no means was his degree of admiration of Iriarte universal at that time. Much of our first chapter, and the succeeding ones, will deal with this apparent paradox in the career of Tomás de Iriarte. That he could evoke both extremes of love and hatred is a major fact of his life, and it is the aspect that essentially molds his personality as a writer. The purpose of this chapter, then, will be to show what occurred in his life that caused both favorable and unfavorable reactions among his contemporaries and, more important, how people aroused certain reactions in him.

Iriarte was born on September 18, 1750, in Puerto de la Cruz on Tenerife, one of the Canary Islands. He was the youngest son of Bernardo de Iriarte and Bárbara de las Nieves de Oropesa;

his brothers were Bernardo, Juan Tomás, Domingo, and José. It was to his uncle, Juan de Iriarte, that Tomás owed the good turn of events that caused him to go to the Spanish mainland. The uncle's importance for Tomás' career merits certain recollections of his own life.

Juan de Iriarte was at a very early age sent to Paris for his education, and later in other parts of France his avid interest in letters began to mature. At the Collège de Louis-le-Grand (where Voltaire was also a pupil) he studied principally languages, philosophy, and mathematics. It was here too that he read and studied the writers of Antiquity who became his mentors for the remainder of his life. Except for a short stay on Tenerife he spent most of the rest of his life in Madrid where he moved in 1724. Evidently he originally intended to follow a career in law, but he became so interested in the holdings of the Royal Library that he never really made a serious attempt to disregard his call to the field of letters. Receiving the attention first of the head librarian and then of the Dukes of Béjar and Alba, by 1732 he had become an official member of the library staff. This position was doubly important to him, for, in addition to allowing him to live with financial security, it gave him more time for his favorite pursuits: criticism, philology, and bibliography. Juan de Iriarte soon became an outstanding literary critic. In 1737 the influential literary review *Diario de los literatos de España (Diary of the Writers of Spain)* first appeared and Iriarte was a frequent contributor. His first article in this journal was a review of Father Jacinto Segura's *Norte crítico, con las reglas más ciertas para la discreción en la historia (Critical Guide, Containing the Most Certain Rules for Discretion in History)*, which had been first printed in 1733. Segura was a harsh critic of Feijoo, and Iriarte in his article takes Segura to task for what he considers unfair criticism.

Ultimately Juan de Iriarte found himself enmeshed in the polemic between the anti- and pro-Feijoo camps. In 1747 he became a member of the Royal Academy of the Language, where he continued his participation in the composing and editing of the Academy's *Grammar* and *Dictionary*. As curator of manuscripts in the Royal Library he compiled a careful and complete Index, gathered material for his *Bibliotheca graeca (Greek Library)*, composed an essay on *Paleografía griega (Greek Paleog-*

[16]

raphy), as well as other no less worthy endeavors. He wrote a
great deal of poetry in Latin, which seems to have been a kind
of relaxation for him. Being quick of mind, he was an excellent
composer of epigrams. He wrote some seven hundred of his own,
translated more than one hundred by other composers into Latin,
and rendered more than two hundred of Martial's into Spanish.
In 1754 he was made director of a project to produce a Latin-
Spanish dictionary, but in 1758, due to illness and overwork, he
was forced to withdraw from this task. Unfortunately the dictionary was never finished. At the same time that he was laboring
on these projects he was working on his *Gramática latina, escrita
con nuevo método y nuevas observaciones, en verso castellano,
con su explicación en prosa (Latin Grammar, Written With a New
Method and New Observations, in Spanish Verse, With Explanations in Prose)*, which he never saw published although it was at
the printer's when he died in 1771. Juan's nephews collected and
published his remaining works. This endeavor was made possible
through the generosity of certain nobles and the Princes Gabriel,
Luis, and Antonio. Such a generous act indirectly shows the intimate ties that Juan de Iriarte enjoyed with members of the royal
court.

In a letter to Juan de Iriarte's nephew Bernardo, Father Enrique
Flórez, confessor and friend of the former, gives a good résumé
of what and who Juan de Iriarte was: "But I especially recall
that rare combination of talents which he possessed, that universal
knowledge of everything in particular, that very delicate taste
that intuited the finest in everything, that great humility toward
everything he knew, that mouth whose lips never maligned
anyone . . . that pure and fragile conscience that put God first
and that always both edified and confused me. The suffering,
patience, and resignation which he demonstrated in his last days
in the continuous afflictions with which the Lord purified him
moved me many times, seeing a man of such irreproachable
character beg me to ask God to forgive him." [2] The picture presented here of Tomás de Iriarte's uncle serves several purposes,
the main one being to show the environment in which the nephew
grew up. In this so very eighteenth-century atmosphere, created
and developed by the uncle, the nephew was provided with ideas
and concepts which he would probably not have received otherwise. The help was not merely subtle, for it manifested itself in

more direct, overt ways such as in opportunities for employment
and for acceptance in both the social and literary fields. It was
this ready-made road which helped Tomás de Iriarte so quickly
to gain national and, eventually, international acclaim. For these
reasons the above portrait of the uncle is necessary. Without it we
shall understand less of the nephew's early progress in the new
world he found in peninsular Spain.

Of the five sons born to Bernardo de Iriarte and his wife
Bárbara de las Nieves de Oropesa three went on to establish
their names in either diplomacy or letters. The two who remained
at home did nothing to distinguish themselves. Domingo, Bernardo, and Tomás were the three who set forth in a new direction.
Bernardo is really a fascinating figure not so much for what he
himself did but for the way he influenced his brother Tomás,
and in many ways helped establish the latter's reputation before
and after his death. Bernardo (born in 1735) was the first of the
Iriarte sons to go to Madrid to live with their uncle, Juan. The
latter very soon had him involved in his own literary projects and
helped him obtain certain political posts. Bernardo was a prodi-
gious worker, involving himself principally in politics and diplomacy. In 1760 he was named Secretary at the Spanish embassy in
London, and, when this position terminated because of the hos-
tilities between England and Spain in the 1760's, he returned to
Madrid where he was connected with the Department of State.
Being a dilettante of sorts he dabbled in writing by publishing
prose versions of some Latin poems of his uncle. He also had a
great propensity for collecting paintings, a pastime that made him
the owner of one of the better-known galleries in Europe. But
it was his devotion to the name of the family that most deserves
comment. He was principally the one responsible for the publication of his uncle's works after the latter's death in 1771. More
pertinent to our own study, Bernardo constantly counseled his
brother Tomás on what and even when he should write. He was
the most ardent admirer that his brother had, a not unworthy fact
since it was Bernardo de Iriarte who directed the excellent posthumous edition of Tomás' works which appeared in eight volumes
in 1805. It would not be amiss to say that Bernardo served very
much as a father to Tomás, especially after Juan de Iriarte's death.
Such a relationship may have unconsciously affected the development of the younger brother since some of his compulsive actions

are greatly reminiscent of those of Bernardo. Bernardo was the last of the three brothers to die, ending his life somewhat as he had lived it—with a certain bitterness and rancor in exile in France. Serving as a counterpoint to Bernardo was Domingo de Iriarte, born in 1739. Although not so well endowed intellectually as the oldest brother, he was much calmer and less ambitious. During his life he held several diplomatic posts.

II *Tomás de Iriarte in His Youth*

Destined to be the most famous of all the children, Tomás de Iriarte was the last of the five to be born, on September 18, 1750, as we saw earlier. He was baptized in the church of Puerto de la Cruz on September 27, 1750, with the name of Tomás Francisco Agustín, his godfather being his brother and future teacher, Juan Tomás.[3] At the age of ten he left the small port town and went inland the few miles to La Orotava where he was taught by his brother. He learned Latin precociously and wrote in that language at a very early age. Several sources report that when he left for Madrid in 1764 he wrote some Latin verses bidding farewell to his birthplace. Fernández Navarrete has the most straightforward and concise account of this occurrence: ". . . [he] left Santa Cruz in early 1764 and bade farewell to his homeland with some Latin distichs, which were not thought possible from a person so young."[4] On coming to live with his uncle he immediately began his education in Madrid complementing what he had already studied at home with Greek, French, sciences, and the Spanish classics. Again we see the strength of the influence Juan de Iriarte exerted on the formation of his nephew. The varied background to which Tomás was exposed at this early and receptive age was bound to mold him into a versatile, open-minded individual. This formal schooling so ably directed by the uncle could only have a beneficent result. Tomás' pleasure in writing poetry was advanced at this time by the composition of a ballad, really of no great consequence except that it shows the early direction of his talents. This interest in poetry was continued in other compositions of about the same period: translations of works of Fontenelle and of Father Porée. More than likely, these were tasks assigned by Juan de Iriarte. However, two works of this time (*ca.* 1765) were probably written independently. These were a Latin poem with its translation into the Spanish *silva* concerning

the masked balls in Madrid and another Latin poem later translated into Spanish called *La fiera ruidosa del Gevaudan en Francia*
(*The Noisome Beast Gevaudan of France*). This latter was probably based on a similarly titled French poem about a strange
animal found in Languedoc that badly frightened the populace
in the mid-1760's.[5]

Iriarte next moved into the field of drama but his appearance
there took a more indirect route. In the 1760's the Spanish theater
began to undergo its restoration so loudly demanded by the
more French-inclined writers and critics. Two events hastened the
change. The first was the death in 1767 of the popular actress
María Ladvenant whose loss to the public, already divided between her admirers and her detractors, only heightened the uproar her acting had at times occasioned. The second event was the
decision of the Count of Aranda, Spain's Prime Minister, to make
the physical appearance of the productions more pleasant and to
provide the public with more and better entertainment. More important for the dramatists themselves was his decision to carry
out the long-desired reform in the style of the drama. He began
by soliciting opinions from the literati of the day, among whom
was Bernardo de Iriarte. Bernardo, while continuing diligently in
the field of diplomacy, was becoming more and more productive
in the literary field. Among other things, in 1765 he published
a translation in Spanish verse of Voltaire's *Tancrède*. In 1764 he
had been elected a member of the Academy. Aranda gave him
the task of searching out those dramas which most closely followed Classic precepts. Of some six hundred Golden Age plays
which he examined, seventy were chosen to be presented in the
capital. Bernardo altered some of these works before presentation,
going a little beyond Aranda's directives. He even went so far
as to suggest that some contemporary writers quit producing their
own works and merely translate French plays. He further suggested, more reasonably, that the presentation of *sainetes* between
acts be abandoned and from here he launched into a harsh attack on this genre in general. Aranda, feeling these and other
suggestions might be better received outside Madrid at first, established theaters at all the royal residences. In 1768 the *Teatros
Reales de los Sitios* thus came into existence.[6]

Tomás de Iriarte translated a rather large number of plays for
these theaters between 1769 and 1772, probably inspired thereto

by Juan de Iriarte. Those done in prose were written thus because it was thought they would be more pleasing to the Spanish in that form. However, when Iriarte's works were collected and published in 1787, all of these plays were excluded precisely because they were in prose. Two in verse were published: *El filósofo casado (The Married Philosopher)* by Destouches and *El huérfano de la China (The Chinese Orphan)* by Voltaire. Of all the translations these two plays were the only ones ever printed with the translator's own name.

It was not long, however, before Tomás began composing on his own. He was moved by the polemics over the introduction and influence of the French Neoclassic theater to write a play that would follow the rules and would at the same time criticize some vice. The idea of Horace's *utile dulci* (to teach and entertain at the same time) was a standard precept in his mind by this time. The result of his motivation was a play entitled *Hacer que hacemos (The Busybody)*, 1770. It was printed under the anagram of Tirso Imareta and criticized a type—called *fachenda* by the common people—who pretends to be always busy but in reality never does anything. The play appeared in published form because Iriarte was unable to get it produced on the stage. The author thought the person most responsible for this rejection was the popular *sainetero* Ramón de la Cruz, whom Iriarte considered the greatest obstacle to a true renovation of the Spanish theater.

In this same year (1770) the declaration of the "new theater" was made manifest by the performance of Nicolás Fernández de Moratín's *Hormesinda*. The production of this play was greatly helped by Aranda's influence. For all practical purposes this event may be considered the date of the beginning of the public clash between the Neoclassicists and the Traditionalists (these latter being best represented by Ramón de la Cruz). Verbal blows were lustily exchanged between the two camps, and it must be said that Ramón de la Cruz appears to have been most lenient before reacting against his enemies. Indicating early his unfortunate propensity to respond compulsively in public quarrels, Iriarte declared himself on the side of Moratín although not in too warm a fashion. His critique is contained in a document called *Carta escrita al Pardo por un caballero de Madrid a un amigo suyo (Letter Written by a Gentleman of Madrid to His Friend)*.

The letter is long and is divided into two parts. The quotation we take from it shows that, although Iriarte delighted in becoming involved in this type of polemic, he was able to maintain a sense of justice and courtesy—qualities not, unfortunately, evident in his enemies. He writes: " 'To say *Hormesinda* is an excellent drama is to lie; to say it has nothing good in it is to exaggerate; to make an absolute apology for it is to proceed with little intelligence; to condemn it entirely in each one of its parts is to proceed with much passion. Having established, therefore, this middle ground . . . you can infer dispassionately, not that it is a perfect work, but that its author can compose another better one if he subjects himself to others' censure and his own sense of polish.' " [7] There is nothing here of petulance or of snobbery, only a desire to give a just opinion on a subject that greatly concerned Iriarte and his future plans.

Within the Iriarte household after 1771 there was a decided change in the relationship of the three brothers. The death of the uncle, Juan de Iriarte, united them even more closely than before. Bernardo became more or less the head of the family while advancing solidly in his employ in the State Department. Domingo continued in this same division of the government. Tomás, who until this time had not held a public position, was named Official Translator of the Secretariat of State, a post formerly held by his uncle. Interestingly, at this same time he composed a poem in Latin (and Spanish) on the founding of the Order of Charles III established in honor and celebration of the birth of the son of the future Charles IV. Whether or not the composition of the poem was meant as a political gesture, its appearance could only enhance the stature of Iriarte who was now progressing quite well. In 1772 Iriarte was given the directorship of the gazette *Mercurio*. He introduced innovations in the already well-established but bland periodical by giving space to much of what went on outside Spain, a practice not very tenaciously followed up to that time. It soon became evident, however, that Iriarte was not much interested in the mechanics of journalism, and after less than a year he asked to be relieved of his duties. The directorship was turned over to Clavijo y Fajardo, who was also the director of the royal theaters. The new director lacked Iriarte's talent for new ideas and as a result the periodical never again rose above a certain mediocrity.

It was becoming increasingly popular to publish short essays or papers in a series that censured or criticized literary and scientific works, events of the time, or certain customs of the people. The best-known work of this type is Cadalso's *Los eruditos a la violeta (The Superficial Erudites)*, a very sharp, incisive literary satire which perhaps influenced Iriarte a year later (1773) to write *Los literatos en cuaresma (Writers in Lent)*. During the early 1770's Iriarte and Cadalso were very close friends. They were both intimately associated with the Fonda de San Sebastián where one of the most important *tertulias* met. It was here that they, along with others, recited or read selections from their published and unpublished works. The *tertulia* functioned as a kind of editorial board because in some cases, evidently according to its reception there, a passage might be later added to or omitted from a work to be published. It is known that Iriarte, for example, made certain observations here on the musical qualities of the Spanish language—observations which strangely were not amplified later in his poem *La música (Music)*. The cordial relationship between Iriarte and Cadalso was significant for various reasons. Having much the same likes and dislikes, their reactions were often similar, and from the 1770's on there was a large correspondence between them while Cadalso was in the countryside away from the capital. They both had keen wit and deep insight and were able to comment significantly on the life around them. Iriarte's letters are in a way the more valuable because he writes to Cadalso about events in Madrid. The major portion of his correspondence concerns literary events and the resultant criticism on both sides of a controversy. Cadalso serves as a stimulus for Iriarte's thoughts when he begs for news since, on duty as a soldier, he feels lost in a wasteland. Iriarte, his replies being accurate commentaries on contemporary people and occurrences, acts much in the way of a diarist. These letters were not extensively investigated until the efforts of Cotarelo and Foulché-Delbosc in 1894–1895.[8]

While actively engaged in his literary activities Iriarte continued advancing his more social and political aims, although politics was left more to his two brothers. Bernardo, who was steadily progressing in the State Department, was elected a member of the Academy of San Fernando in 1774. Domingo was appointed Secretary to the embassy in Vienna in 1776, a post he held for about ten years. Tomás was named Archivist of the Supreme Council of War on May 24, 1776. He officially took the post on July 31. Soon after, he wrote a *Memoria* recounting the state of the Archives and proposing some reforms he considered necessary. This position with that of Official Translator for the State gave him a certain influence and social position that he found quite attractive. From most accounts he was greatly beloved by his friends and even distant acquaintances. According to Cotarelo, his personal attributes included "a graceful and agreeable figure, a face that, without being precisely handsome, had energy and a little mocking expression which his portrait reveals. Agile in all kinds of bodily exercise, he prided himself on being a good fencer and an indefatigable dancer. . . . There should be added to this his great competence in the musical art, which, as we have seen, was one of his great hobbies." [9] We may add the words of a contemporary to the effect that he "had a naturally frank and agreeable wit. He was sought out at all gatherings, and his society was no less pleasing to men than to women." [10] In addition to the foregoing attributes, his poetic abilities were widely appreciated and caused him to be one of the most outstanding figures of young Madrid society. His ability to improvise verses so easily provided him immediate entry to the most fashionable gatherings. Also a natural taste for dressing luxuriously and elegantly combined with a special fondness for attending the more aristocratic functions aided him in gaining entrance to just about any salon he wished to be a part of.

One of the households in which Iriarte was most cordially received was that of the Duke of Villahermosa, Juan Pablo de Aragón y Azlor, and his young wife, María Manuela Pignatelli y Gonzaga. Bernardo and Tomás de Iriarte were more than just occasional visitors in this rather lively home. Iriarte had been the music teacher of the Duchess, whom he affectionately called Manolita, and had actively participated in the musicales held in her house. These gatherings were interrupted in 1776 because of the death of the Duchess's father, the Count of Fuentes, and were terminated completely in 1778 when the Duke was named ambassador to Turin. Iriarte did maintain an active correspondence with this couple, however, and again, much as in the letters to Cadalso, he tells many pertinent details about the life of the times. In these letters, however, there is much more about his own troubles as he becomes increasingly involved in polemics inspired by his newest works. From the relationship with this couple came others with their relatives, perhaps the most important of whom for our purposes in studying his life was Carlos Pignatelli, brother of the Duchess. He is important in that he wrote a very good critique of Iriarte's life that unfortunately did not see publication until 1916 (see note number 10). His biographical and critical sketch was to have been printed at the beginning of the 1805 edition of Iriarte's works. Bernardo de Iriarte, believing much of what Pignatelli wrote was too blunt and might revive old quarrels, refused to include it, however. The work remained in oblivion—Cotarelo even thought it lost—until Antonio Aguirre published it.

At the home of the Marquis of Castelar Iriarte enjoyed other than purely literary pastimes, for here equestrian contests which were so popular at the time were frequently held. Tomás often caustically satirized these gatherings, the people who attended them, and what they did. An even greater friendship developed between Iriarte and the Marquis of Manca, Manuel Delitala. The Marquis was young and already was involved in diplomatic missions, but it was his delight in music which brought him and Iriarte together. In his home musicales were also held and Iriarte was a frequent and major participant. The two wrote each other in both prose and verse when one or the other was away from the city. They even had nicknames for each other based on certain peculiarities they had when playing music. Iriarte was called *Camaſeo* (based on *cameo*) because of his appearance when giving a recital, and Delitala was called *Ronquido* because of a strange rasping sound in his throat that the difficult passages of Haydn elicited from him.

Even more important to the Iriartes was the appointment of the Count of Floridablanca, José Moñino, as Prime Minister on February 19, 1777. Bernardo looked upon the ascension of Floridablanca as the means to attain the political power he had so long desired and envisioned. To enhance his already substantial position and bring himself more to the attention of Floridablanca, he directed himself more openly to the question of the annexation of Portugal. In 1762 shortly after his return from London he had worked on the translation of a pamphlet in French entitled *Profecía política (Political Prophecy)* that dealt with the problem

of Portugal. It was published but went out of print that same year
and was not reprinted until 1808. Now in 1777 Bernardo himself
wrote another *Discurso (Discourse)* on Portugal advocating the
immediate conquest of Portugal, thus avoiding a "marriage" or
other equally acceptable methods but admittedly more complicated. Through such a conquest by Spain, Bernardo hoped to
see the total end of all English influence in the Iberian Peninsula.
Perhaps because of his disappointed diplomatic hopes in London,
Bernardo had become particularly disenchanted with the English
and was determined to do them damage in whatever feasible way
he could. Such ardent nationalism met with the approval of
Floridablanca, who then began to grant him much consideration,
not the least of which was the appointment of Bernardo as Secretary to the King. As a bonus, Domingo was also advanced but
did not leave the embassy in Vienna. Tomás more or less joined
the act by presenting Floridablanca with a work to which he had
recently devoted himself, his translation of Horace's *Poetics.*

III   Iriarte's Coming of Age

In his *Epístola IX, escrita en 20 de mayo de 1776 (Espistle IX,
Written May 20, 1776)* Iriarte confesses that his truest friend was
always Horace: "Horace is my library;/ And his books contain so
much,/ That the more I read in them/ The less I feel I have read."
*(Horacio es mi biblioteca;/ Y encierran tanto sus libros,/ Que
quanto mas léo en ellos/ Ménos créo haber leido.)* [11] The result
of this admiration and devotion was the translation of Horace's
Poetics or *Epistle to the Pisones*, which appeared in 1777. From
this date on Iriarte was involved more and more publicly in his
writing. That is to say, he truly began to concern himself with the
polemics that were to consume so much of his time and energy
during the rest of his life. As would be the case later when others
of his works were published, there was praise of his translation of
Horace but the negative criticism was just loud enough to mo-
tivate his retort. As if in a circle, and a vicious one at that, his
reply only goaded on his critics to more vociferous attacks. From
here on much of what Iriarte wrote was often in direct response
to the unfavorable criticism of his work. Whether this was a
legitimate motivation is not our duty to decide. It does seem that
much of this (to us) childish arguing on both sides could have
been avoided. Yet such polemics were an inherent part of the

literary and cultural scene in general, not only of eighteenth-century Spain but of the rest of Europe as well. To fail to notice this propensity for polemics would be to omit a substantial part of what is most essential to the eighteenth-century mentality.[12]

When the translation was published several critiques appeared, both positive and negative, as the author had expected. Iriarte wrote a *Carta familiar y apologética en satisfacción a varios reparos sobre la nueva traducción del Arte poética de Horacio (Familiar and Apologetic Letter to Satisfy Several Observations Concerning the New Translation of the Poetics of Horace)*. In it he says he is writing to the favorable critics and not the negative ones who are conveniently dismissed as unproductive themselves yet delighting in destroying others' efforts. These latter critics had censured him for admittedly rather petty reasons: that it was not difficult to translate the *Poetics* since translations and commentaries already existed, that Iriarte's version was too tedious and redundant, and that it was not really his own work but that of his uncle.

The upshot of all this unnecessary bickering was that Iriarte ended up in a long, bitter tirade with Juan José López de Sedano, who had only recently introduced his grandiose collection, the *Parnaso español (Spanish Parnassus)*, with Vicente Espinel's translation of the *Poetics*. The Espinel translation was poor, having been done more as a student exercise than as a truly scholarly endeavor. Its numerous errors were what irritated Iriarte most. That he should attack its inclusion in a collection which was to be comprised of the most outstanding productions of the Spanish literary genius was not at all unexpected. At the publication of the ninth volume of the *Parnassus* in July, 1778, Sedano made comments about some remarks of Iriarte in the prologue to his own translation of Horace. Sedano could not defend his previous position concerning Espinel and the reasons for including him in his work, so he resorted to attacks on Iriarte's translation. Among other things, he said Iriarte had committed many errors in interpretation, but interestingly enough Sedano cited none of these so-called errors. Iriarte almost immediately replied in a satire called *Donde las dan las toman (Give and Take)* published in the fall of 1778. Two letters of Vicente de los Ríos, the commentator of *Don Quixote*, were included in this treatise and soon involved him as well in this unfortunate squabble. Showing the lengths to which these polemics often became involved, the events here are extremely enlightening. Ríos had formerly been the friend of Sedano but on taking Iriarte's side in this matter Ríos was immediately attacked. Not only was he attacked at this time, but even after his death he was not freed from the vicious tongue of Sedano. In 1785 Sedano published a work called *Coloquios de la espina (Colloquies of the Spine)*. Ostensibly it was a continuation of the attack on Iriarte, but in the fourth volume he really lambasts Ríos.[13] It was a fear of this sort of snide irreverence that prompted Bernardo de Iriarte to omit Pignatelli's sketch from the edition of his brother's works in 1805.

In regard to the Iriarte-Sedano episode, it can be said that for once one of these all-too-common eighteenth-century polemics produced a work of some merit—*Give and Take*. The tone employed by Iriarte is temperate. His criticism is not at first directed at the editor but at the work. He at the end says he has nothing against Sedano other than this literary dispute. He for one is not willing to make himself an enemy of Sedano simply because he disagrees with his choice of works. One result of all this bickering was the demise of the *Spanish Parnassus*. No more volumes appeared. This perhaps unexpected outcome might have been avoided if the series had had a more capable editor than Sedano. Again one is somewhat overwhelmed by the capriciousness of eighteenth-century writers and editors. Had they all been better able to hold their tongues, we might today possess an even greater production from them. As a final note on this event, Iriarte received much praise for his dialogue, even from Floridablanca. It is conceivable therefore that the results of these public arguments were not always bad for everyone.

Two events occurred in 1777–1778 that had influence on Iriarte's life. The first had nothing really to do with guiding his actions, but it was important in its implications of what was to happen to him at the end of the next decade. Pablo de Olavide came to Madrid from Lima and almost immediately became a favorite of influential governmental circles. He married well and had the protection of Aranda, who gave him the responsibility for founding the colonies of the Sierra Morena, a project pushed by the government to reclaim poor lands and to resettle hitherto unfortunate citizens in a completely new environment. Olavide became very powerful in Andalusia because, although he possessed quite aristocratic tastes, he was most democratic in his ideas. Perhaps he was too democratic, for in 1778 he was brought before the Inquisition and accused of maintaining a dissolute household. The Inquisition showed itself to be far from moribund by, for all practical purposes, exiling Olavide from all he had previously known and taking away all his wealth. It was not until 1798 that he was allowed to return from France—an old, broken man.[14] The Inquisition would in about ten years push its way into the life of Tomás de Iriarte, but fortunately not in quite so blunt and unsympathetic a way.

The other event was the Royal Academy's establishment in 1777 of its literary competitions. The contests themselves were important, not so much for the works that were produced for them but for the fact that they called for material commemorating events of national glory and renown. This awakening of interest in the past—and a certain glorification of it—goes hand in hand with the publication of many of the literary monuments of the past (witness Tomás Antonio Sánchez and his labors). In the first competition in 1777 the subject proposed for prose was a eulogy of Philip V, the intention being to praise the king responsible for the founding of the Academy. A poem on Cortez' destruction of his ships was the theme for poetry. This theme was felt to be most heroic, an attitude coming much into vogue among the literati who thought such a stance capable of prodding the Spanish into a more lofty literary production. Forty-five compositions were presented in the poetry division. Men of recognized reputation participated, but the prize (presented on August 13, 1778) went to an unknown poet, José María Vaca de Guzmán y Derechos.

In the competition in 1778 Leandro Fernández de Moratín, aged nineteen, presented a composition but was defeated by Vaca, who was again victorious. Moratín did receive the second prize. Iriarte had somewhat veiled intentions of participating in 1778; however, he was probably pushed to participate more by his friends than by himself. In a letter to Enrique Ramos of May 11, 1779, he wrote: "'. . . you [Enrique Ramos] tell me to write something for the prizes offered by the Spanish Academy, but you should know that I do not wish to undertake so much. I shall make my ingenuous confession: . . . I declare that I do not feel in me the impulses of truly epic enthusiasm. How could that be!'"

(The theme for the contest in poetry was the conquest of Granada.) He continues with: "'Yes, my friend, I assure you that only for satire do I have that genius which inspires verses worthy of being left for posterity.'"[15] Even though he did not enter the competition for 1778, he did present an entry for that of 1779. The theme for poetry was a praise of country life to be written in an eclogue of five hundred to six hundred lines. Iriarte's eclogue was entitled appropriately *La felicidad de la vida del campo (The Happiness of Country Life)*. He chose a pseudonym, Francisco Agustín de Cisneros, thus employing his second name and the surname of his grandmother. The only thing he said about himself was that he was an "old Castilian." The work which was awarded the prize was *Batilo*, a bucolic poem by Juan Meléndez Valdés.

Unfortunately, Iriarte, who had initially disclaimed all interest in the prize ("'[the old Castilian, i.e., Iriarte] does not aspire to the prize, but only the satisfaction of meriting the indulgence of the Academy.'"),[16] showed himself dissatisfied with the judges' decision by publishing some *Reflexiones sobre la égloga de Batilo (Reflections Concerning the Eclogue Batilo)*. The extent of his displeasure was obviously considerable, for this work occupies some sixty-seven pages of the last volume of the 1805 edition of his works. The significant thing for us, however, is what happened afterward. To take a position greatly different from Iriarte's, a most virulent critic arrived on the scene. This was Juan Pablo Forner. It was he who was to cause Iriarte so much trouble for the rest of his life. Eventually an outstanding writer of the time, he is more remembered today because of the polemics in which he took such great delight. Almost no writer, great or insignificant, was safe from his diatribes. The target most often was the person of the writer and not his work. Needless to say, his manner of writing was bound to produce a public for him—a public which he was hardly loath to accept. The work he wrote against Iriarte at this time was called *Cotejo de las églogas que ha premiado la Real Academia de la Lengua (Comparison of the Eclogues Awarded Prizes by the Royal Academy of the Language)*. Fernando Lázaro has made an excellent edition of this work and in it presents some ideas about Iriarte that are relatively unbiased. Heretofore in the polemic between Iriarte and Forner, critics have tended to take sides so vociferously that they have damaged their own arguments. In addition, they have usually made either Iriarte or Forner seem like an ogre. Lázaro quite sensibly contrasts the positions of the two writers in 1780. Iriarte was reaching the zenith in his literary production; he was the idol of the salons; and he wielded considerable social and political influence. Forner was practically unknown but most desirous of not remaining in that state: "Tomás de Iriarte was the unanimously favored poet. Hardly did a work leave his hands before all Madrid was praising his genius. . . . How very much must Juan Pablo have desired and how much must he have rejoiced at the decision of the Academy. . . . And then the incredible happened: Tomás rebelled against the decision, edited his absurd *Reflections* against Meléndez and had them circulated. Now indeed the anger of Forner had a justifiable pretext. Calling on all the resources of his patience, dampening his wrathful arguments with rational precepts, he wrote the *Comparison*." [17]

Lázaro quotes Forner in one place giving a very good picture of the venom that he held in store for Iriarte. It also indicates how this type of polemic could go beyond any sense of propriety and decency. Since by attacking the person he considered the arbiter of literary tastes of the day he hoped to establish a comfortable niche for himself in Madrid society, Forner is all the more vitriolic in his diatribe:

"Tomás de Iriarte, I say again, elevated by his presumption, has been and is today the greatest obstruction to the advancement of Spanish letters. . . . Persuaded that only the works of his genius or those which come out under his protection can deserve the appreciation of the people, he treats all writers as barbarians, uneducated, crude, and cries out in a loud voice that their works should be prohibited from the literary world. . . . I decided, therefore, to make the author appear ridiculous, taking up his own type of arms. I observed his studies and character, and I found that in addition to not knowing any science, he was even destitute of the slightest knowledge of ancient and modern philosophy (knowledge which the women of France have today) and completely unaware of all that is solid or profound. . . . I became very angry on seeing that, the Spanish Academy having chosen for first place the Eclogue of a friend of mine [Meléndez Valdés], giving only second prize to another which later was found to be Tomás de Iriarte's, the latter became furious and wrote a pamphlet which he and his brother began to spread around in order to discredit, if they could, the genius of my friend and the judgment of the *unlearned* Academy. So to repress him a little and to show that, poetics being the art in which he most glories, he does not even know what an eclogue is, I wrote an analysis of his and the one which received first place; but I did not try to print it for several reasons, contenting myself with showing it to some friends." [18]

In the midst of all this furor, Iriarte completed a work that has never been fully appreciated although it did gain much renown, more outside of Spain than within, when it first appeared in 1780. This work was his poem *La música (Music)* finished in May, 1779. Bernardo succeeded in getting Floridablanca to sponsor its publication. Viera y Clavijo describes at some length the elegance of the edition: "This book in large octavo, with six excellent plates (one of those [books] which have most advanced the progress of the art of printing and engraving in Spain), not only has been for this reason a present worthy of the greatest princes, but in foreign countries many papers rushed to announce it to the European public with particular applause." [19] Pignatelli writes of the work in equally laudatory terms: "At the beginning of 1780 he published one of those works which honor a writer and the nation of which the author who writes it is a citizen. I speak of the poem *Music,* one of our writings of the past century which has merited the greatest applause and is more known among foreigners." [20]

The reputation of the book was indeed tremendous in foreign countries. Translations were made of it in English, French, German, and Italian, and most foreign critics were unstinting in their praise of the book as a literary masterpiece. In Spain it was accepted with relative indifference, a fact which is all the more curious given the aesthetic quality of the book. Cotarelo quotes a heretofore unpublished letter of Juan Antonio Pellicer, the commentator of *Don Quixote,* that shows this intriguing lack of interest in the new work. The letter indirectly notes the acclaim the poem received elsewhere when Pellicer mentions Metastasio's genuine interest in Iriarte's new production: " 'Tomás de Iriarte has just published his didactic poem *Music,* with elegant and luxurious engravings: a work new for Spain and even for Europe, it is said, and which has merited the praise of Metastasio who has already read a copy and understands notoriously well our language and music in general. He has explained his judgment saying that [the work] approaches the sublime and he marvels at the fact that both Iriarte and he have coincided in some observations and discoveries, since Metastasio, it appears, is going to publish the *Poetics* of Aristotle in Italian, with notes concerning music.' " [21]

It is again Pignatelli who most succinctly explains the reason for the lack of interest in general in Spain and even the open animosity the poem awoke in some segments of Madrid society: "The publication of the poem *Music* was the period of enmity and rancor of several literati and pretenders against Tomás de Iriarte. At that time there was formed a kind of league which was called the Anti-Iriartistas. . . . The true motive for this enmity has been discovered, that is, a secret envy of the literary reputation with which Iriarte was advancing, since a man like him who cultivated letters because he liked to, who respected the public and all writers good or bad . . . could not gain enemies except through the motives indicated [i.e., jealousy and envy]. . . ." [22]

While these polemics were developing, particularly the one between Forner and Iriarte mentioned before—a polemic that would never leave Iriarte in peace and that would affect his personality and his remaining works in many ways, the Iriarte brothers continued to advance in the social and political fields. This advancement was exactly the type of power that Forner so coveted and that pressed him to write against the Iriartes. Bernardo, the oldest official in point of service in the State Department became Councilor, being appointed the successor to Fernando Magallón in the division for the Indies. He was still a great favorite of the Prime Minister, and it was Bernardo who inspired Floridablanca to establish a general Academy of Arts and Sciences. About the only definite thing that came of his recommendations was a building, the present Prado Museum. In some unedited material of several years later Bernardo goes on at great length about this project. His remarks are interesting too for the rather petulant attitude he exhibits toward Floridablanca, who had always done the utmost to help him:

"The Minister had been in power some years (three or four), when with great difficulty, I persuaded him to promote the establishment of an Academy of Sciences, stimulating him with the idea that there had never been a successful Minister who had not promoted such. . . . He adopted the idea and wanted my brother Tomás de Iriarte, whom he flattered many years with vain hopes, and whose genius, penetration and superior logic frightened him, to formulate the plan of the Academy, as in effect he did. . . . Some time later he decided to construct a building in the Prado for the future Academy. He thought of the building, but not of the scholars either present or future because he was afraid of them and did not care for them, especially the first ones, because they always eclipsed him and disturbed him during his ministry, and he humiliated them, exalting the stupid and ignorant. . . . Later, in the reign of Charles IV, the Count of Floridablanca repeated to me one day in his house after dinner the same question he had asked on becoming Minister; that is, what was my opinion. 'You have lost much precious time,' I said to him. 'How many things you might have done which you did not do in the reign of Charles III! I do not know whether you will be able to do them at present. . . . You intended to establish an Academy of Sciences, and instead of bringing together the scholars, although it might have been in a garret, you ordered a place to be built for them in the Prado. The building is still to be finished and meanwhile one (that of the Inquisition) is about to be completed near where you live in order to shut them up [the scholars].' The Count became quiet, and I took my leave and went home leaving him that little *post café*. After the fall of the Count I found out from someone in the State Department that that Minister, notwithstanding his having indicated to me approval of the plan proposed by my brother Tomás, had passed it reservedly to the most reverend Father Villalpando; this latter, disapproving of said plan, proposed a very foolish one. . . ." 23

In 1780 Iriarte had indeed written a *Plan de una Academia de Ciencias y Bellas Letras (Plan for an Academy of Sciences and Letters)* at the request of Floridablanca. On August 8, 1780, he sent his ideas to the Count accompanying his proposals with some *Reflexiones sueltas (Miscellaneous Reflections)* and *Consideraciones que se han tenido presentes para la extensión del plan de la Academia de Ciencias y Buenas* [sic] *Letras (Considerations For the Extension of the Plan)*, and the constitutions of other Academies such as those of Berlin, St. Petersburg, and Lisbon. The *Considerations* are of no outstanding value since most of the ideas are found elsewhere in his works—in particular, the translating of the best of foreign works and the establishment of a censorial board for books. However, the *Reflections* are more valuable since they give some interesting ideas concerning writers as professionals and the public's reaction to them: " 'Here it is

believed that an author produces a book as a tree does leaves;
and when they see that those who write not only do not arrive
thereby to any high estate, but even do not obtain the where-
withal to eat if they do not abandon literature to occupy themselves in offices, etc., they infer that literature is not a true pro-
fession, or career, or an occupation worthy of a man's killing
himself for it, but a mere diversion, like playing an instrument,
playing games with the hands, playing cards well, etc.' " [24] These
ideas denote a certain irony and disillusionment with the public
as the years passed.

Iriarte's *Plan for an Academy* was organized as follows: the
Academy was to be divided into two sections—Science, with
twenty-six members, and Letters, with twelve. These members
were to be of three types—honorary, salaried professors, and
associates. There were to be corresponding members outside of
Madrid. Of the twelve in Letters three were to devote their time
to Criticism and Literary History, especially that of Spain; three
to Grammar, Rhetoric, and Style; two to Language; two to Poetry;
and two to Antiquities and Inscriptions. Iriarte also slyly inserted a criticism of the Royal Academy for publishing old instead of new works and for publishing a very defective *Grammar,*
principally because its compiler (Ignacio de Luzán) was, he
thought, a man who spent most of his time in an office and because those who revised it were men not totally devoted to the
ardors of such a task. It is interesting to note that Bernardo de
Iriarte in 1796 wrote to Godoy, trying to revive the above plan
by telling him it was he who first suggested the whole matter to
Floridablanca. He sent him copies of the *Plan* and of the *Reflections* of his brother but now modified by himself.[25]

While Iriarte was involved in the more serious endeavors just
mentioned, he continued to play the role of the sophisticated
young gentleman. He never once stopped attending the gatherings or salons of his wealthy, aristocratic friends. One of these
people was the Duchess of Osuna, María Josefa Alfonsa Pimentel
y Téllez-Girón, to whom Iriarte dedicated many of his poems both
serious and comic, all proclaiming her virtues. It was she who had
a theater built wherein two of Iriarte's plays were later presented;
these were *El don de gentes (Winning Ways)* and *Donde menos
se piensa salta la liebre (It Would Happen Where Least Expected).* Perhaps because of the excesses he may have committed

from leading a rather free life in Madrid, Iriarte took a recrea-
tional trip to the provinces in the summer of 1781. He began to
make such trips periodically to improve his health, which was
never very good from this time on. He suffered from that all-too-
common disease of the eighteenth century, gout. He would alter-
nately become ill and then withdraw to a more ascetic life for a
while, seeking to negate the dangers into which he had fallen.
Usually his remedy was successful but as the years passed, he was
to find it increasingly difficult to cure himself. As the illness en-
gulfed him more and more every year, he vainly struggled to keep
his composure and maintain a façade that would hide the pain
he was suffering. He evidently succeeded in this superficial
posture better than he hoped because only a few intimate friends
actually realized what he was suffering, and this only at the end.
At any rate, on this trip in 1781 he set forth much like Don
Quixote (to whom he compared himself), and a quotation is given
here from a letter to Delitala so that his attitude may be seen and
understood—the attitude that would maintain him through all
kinds of misery: " 'On Sunday, 22 of July, at four in the morning,
[occurred] the first departure of Don Quixote, not into the country but on the road to Alcalá, in the company of a Sancho Panza
who because of his simplicity deserved to have his fame per-
petuated in histories just like the other one.' " [26] He then goes on
to narrate other adventures he encountered. He sounds like most
other travelers of that time who found it necessary to move about
the country where roads were impassable, people often inhos-
pitable, and the inns disgustingly unclean. But in all these descriptions there is never lacking a certain humor—granted, at times
a bit caustic—but his attitude indicates that he was able to maintain his composure in spite of what he was feeling. In this same
letter he goes on to narrate the following humorous incident
which so slyly reveals the costumbristic side of his writing:

"Returning to Salceda . . . I have already told you that the Fathers
gave me lodging and dinner; but since the pleasures of this life are not
lasting, my bad luck would have it that so many fleas landed on me
that night that they would not let me sleep. Being thus awake and
hearing matins, I decided to go to the choir loft since I was not sleep-
ing, and make my observations concerning the singing. I got up and
began very cautiously to walk through dark cloisters and corridors

which I did not know. I was determined to reach the choir, but it was impossible because the Fathers, according to the rigid confinement that they observed, had all communication with the interior of the monastery closed. I heard at a distance the voices, which in the silence of the night resounded sadly. The darkness of those cloisters, the narrow passages which I passed through, the many stairs that I went up and down without knowing where I was going, all added to my confusion; and finally I put on my Quixotic bravery to undertake the dangerous adventure of the Matins, which I shall always compare to that of the Fulling Mills. My Sancho Panza was snoring meanwhile, and his snore served me as a guide to return to my room. I tell you [Delitala] that that night was in all ways worthy of Don Quixote." 27

While off on this trip he was not entirely out of touch with events in the capital. Nor does he seem to have completely dismissed from his mind the Academy literary competitions. Still smarting from his rebuff in the last one, he rather obliquely states his refusal to enter the competition for this year. In another letter to Delitala while praising a *romance* the latter had written him, he says: " 'I do say that your ballad is good. If this is not enough, subject it to the scrutiny of those of the *Batilo* and abide by what seems best to you.' " 28 He is sincere in what he says to his friend, but it is obvious that he has little use for the Academy judges. The subject for this season's contest was a "Satire of two to three hundred tercets against vices introduced into Spanish poetry by bad poets." Such a theme should have been extremely agreeable to Iriarte especially since the subject was one that he often elaborated on elsewhere in his writing. It is difficult to imagine him utterly refusing to participate in the competition. If he really did not carry his intention into action, we must understand that he was still quite upset over the results of the previous year. Cotarelo goes so far as to assert that he did actually contemplate entering: "But if Tomás de Iriarte did not resolve ultimately to try his luck in the Academic competition, it can be assumed that he did conceive the intention of doing so, and he even began to carry it out before the Academy determined the type of meter that the satire it was asking for should have. No other origin can be given to a certain rough draft or satirical fragment, which begins with a written imprecation with an unaccustomed verve in our poet." 29 It is impossible to determine definitely whether Iriarte had serious desires to enter the contest, for Cotarelo's words are purely conjectural and he is the only one who even goes far enough to make these statements. Whatever the true situation was, the outcome of the literary competition for that year was extremely ironic and, more than likely, very bitter for Iriarte. The first prize went to his archenemy Juan Pablo Forner for a poem entitled *Sátira contra los vicios introducidos en la poesía castellana (Satire Against the Vices Introduced into Spanish Poetry)*. Perhaps even more ironic was that the second prize for the second time went to Leandro Fernández de Moratín. This outcome was bound to make Iriarte all the more set against Forner and to make Forner rejoice in his triumph indirectly over Iriarte and the group he represented. It would inevitably cause the relations between the two camps to be more bitter and vitriolic without hope of ever really resolving their differences.

IV *Apogee of Iriarte's Popularity*

In 1782 the book appeared that was to give Iriarte his most lasting fame. This was the *Fábulas literarias (Literary Fables)*. It represents the quintessence of Iriarte's ideas concerning literature, being a synthesis of the motivations behind his previous works and those that would follow. The collection of fables contains a motto which is actually the motto for all of Iriarte's works: *Usus vetusto genere, sed rebus novis* (the use of an old genre but with new aims). Cotarelo makes some very good points concerning the motto and what it implies. These statements delve into the essence of Iriarte and his beliefs. To understand what Cotarelo says is to understand what Iriarte was: "Iriarte's genius, looking for a field in which to spread its wings and not finding it in the known literary forms, decided to create new genres, or even among the common ones to move along unexplored paths, with the purpose of freeing itself if only in part from those precepts obtained through formal education which imprisoned and sterilized his imagination, so fresh and rich as few were among the writers of his time. Thus was born the dialogue *Give and Take*, a polemical work, new in form and agreeable and instructive reading; thus the poem *Music*, which he took up after convincing himself that no one had preceded him in a similar undertaking, and thus he produced his celebrated *Literary Fables*." [30]

The purpose of Iriarte's writing the fables was to set up a body of literary precepts—and to point out the most common defects in contemporary works. His ideas are hardly new and neither are they unduly profound. Their value lies rather in their being a convenient source of reference for the incipient writer. The style of the collection, in addition to its following the precepts herein set forth, is pleasant: Iriarte is carrying out albeit obviously, at least painlessly, that so-beloved eighteenth-century dictum, *utile dulci*. It is a Frenchman (Vézinet) who gives a good, concise idea of the *Fables:* "The *Literary Fables* form a critique of poetry; they also form a collection of satires and, at the time, personal satires at that. An ardent polemicist, Iriarte relentlessly berates those who do not adopt the doctrines of our classicists. Against affectation, against pomposity, against extravagance, against confusion, he leads in Spain the combat that Boileau led in France a century earlier. Like Boileau he is an alert and hard censor for all 'penholders.' " [31] In other words, Iriarte was seeking to calm the exuberance and the disorganization still so characteristic of Spanish writing even at this late date in the century. This restraining of the literary temperament had been the avowed purpose of Luzán some forty-five years before. With the *Fables* we see this desire to limit, to perfect, become richer and more rewarding, for in writing his rules, unlike Luzán, Iriarte creates something entirely new. It is this idea of creating and of teaching that is so important. Iriarte does not allow himself to be sterile but revolts against tired and tiresome rules to in turn use these rules and bring forth something alive and exciting. While leading a vanguard, he does not merely preach; he demonstrates what must be done. The willingness and even avid desire to create are the basic, important qualities in Iriarte. This fecundity he possesses causes him to surpass the Boileaus and Luzáns, although few of his contemporaries, and probably few of our own time, would grant this. Yet the basis for such an assertion is all too obvious to be casually dismissed.

The *Fables* were first announced in the *Gaceta* of April 19; we again recall the year as 1782. The collection contained sixty-seven fables and to the posthumous collection of 1805 nine more were added. But it was several years before 1782 that Iriarte had definitely formed his idea to write the fables. It is difficult to establish a precise date, but there are certain indications that make an approximate one possible. Codex V-383 of the National

Library reliably states that several translations from Phaedrus were made in 1777. The codex is entitled *Obras poéticas de don Thomás de Iriarte, entresacadas de algunos de sus manuscritos (Madrid, año de 1780) (Poetical Works of Tomás de Iriarte, Taken From Some of His Manuscripts)*. Both of these dates are significant because the first tells us when he was writing some of the earliest poems and because the second indicates much progress on the entire work before its final publication in 1782. Cotarelo says that the 1780 manuscript was the one the Countess of Benavente had copied for herself. The manuscript contains almost all the known fables and some unedited ones.[32]

The *Fables* were widely acclaimed when they appeared and almost immediately were read throughout Spain. Pignatelli only a few years later was to write: "The Spanish public has done justice to these fables, which will be perhaps the work of Iriarte that most gives him renown in posterity and that will always be read even when the worth of his other works may be dimmed by the passage of time." [33] The nature of the fables, however, not even considering the personality of their author, was such that polemics very soon began. There were quite sarcastic and virulent attacks made on both the compositions and Iriarte's personality. The first to declare himself, quite naturally, in the enemy camp was Forner with a biting work called *El asno erudito (The Erudite Ass)*. So typical of the day and of the caustic, violent temper exhibited by its writers, the composition would now be termed pure libel. If such a work were to appear publicly today, its author would be undeniably punished in the courts. It was announced in the *Gaceta de Madrid* on July 12, 1782, under a pseudonym, Pablo Segarra (actually Forner's second name and surname). Forner himself writes the following comment (seemingly so innocent) about how he came to compose his poem: " 'The vanity and pride grew from day to day in the soul of that man [Iriarte] and it was then when I, impatient now and urged on by a zeal that I judged correct, published the fable of the *Erudite Ass*.' " [34]

Having commented earlier on the polarization of the critics into completely pro- or anti-Forner forces, the present writer finds it difficult to express his opinion without sounding prejudiced also. When one considers Forner's record and reads what he wrote about others (which unhappily is so much of his total production), onc is amazed at the bitterness and obvious hatred this man felt for some of his contemporaries. Whether a cause or a result of the attitude in his works, Forner's personality was hardly one given to winning lasting friends very easily. He was always goaded on by the overwhelming desire to win public acclaim. Very early the direction he took to obtain it was that of a quite hostile attitude calculated to awaken an almost prurient interest in the public. Even more disturbing was the fact that this public was always eager to mock the object of his diatribe's shortcomings, all the more savory when dished up with a biting wit capable at times of destroying its opponent. Cotarelo's following comment leaves no doubt as to the character of the man, a character unfortunately linked to an unpleasant physical appearance: "He was very thin and tall, of an olive complexion, with a grim look because of a squint, with an angry gesture, a voice both loud and raspy, of few words and slovenly in his person. Thus it is that the first sentiment he awakened was one of repulsion; and instead of overcoming these faults, for which he was not really to blame, he gave full rein to his irascible and rancorous character, determined to destroy any good points in others instead of raising and manifesting his own. His first work was a satire: it could not have been anything else." [35] Forner's first years were spent somewhat fruitlessly in seeking a quick success at court. Such attempts were for the most part wasted although they did result in a satire entitled *Contra los vicios de la corte (Against the Vices of the Court)* in which he olympically laments his inability to achieve his goal. Of course, none of the blame for his situation is necessarily his, he would have us believe. He did later achieve the good graces of Floridablanca and Godoy. But the main thing that thwarted his advancing as he so much desired was his acerbic tongue. Because he was so witty he did achieve great renown with the general public. The popularity of his attack on Iriarte was such that his work was widely known and quoted.

As we would expect, having seen how the previous quarrels mushroomed, Iriarte replied to Forner without delay. If only he had been able to demonstrate more patience, much needless foolishness would have been spared the two antagonists and their all-too-eager public. Yet not to expect such volatility in such a case is really not to understand either the antagonists or much of the basic attitude of the eighteenth century in general. Iriarte answered Forner in the form of a letter from a certain Eleuterio

Geta (an invention of Iriarte). The letter, dated July 12 and announced in the *Gaceta* for August 6, 1782, was entitled *Para casos tales suelen tener los maestros oficiales (For Just Such Cases Do They Have Trained Teachers).*

The rapidity with which these diatribes appeared is indicative of the degree of the anger felt by the two contenders. Iriarte takes a lofty, disdainful attitude toward his attacker, an attitude that naturally only increased the jealousy and hatred of Forner. Perhaps Iriarte was aware of this more subtle effect his letter would have and for that reason alone maintained a superior attitude. He implies that an attack such as Forner's does not deserve the attention it gets through criticism, for to criticize the work is only to give it unmerited recognition and honor. Even though his pose is correct, especially since it sounds so much more reasonable than the raging fulminations of Forner, Iriarte was obviously disturbed by the libelous attack. We should understand that he is really having great difficulty in restraining his anger but that it is through this restraint he hopes to gain the public's favor. Surely they will understand that he is the wronged man and can only admire him more seeing how nobly he comports himself in the face of such unjustified slander. The tone of his letter therefore is very much like that of his polemic earlier with Sedano. He does not attack Forner's person but rather criticizes grammatical and stylistic faults in what he has written, giving erudite and interesting asides when he deems them proper. He does not refer to Forner other than with the initials of his name. He says nothing of Forner's life or habits, at all times therefore showing himself to be the moderate, even-tempered person the really correct eighteenth-century man was presumed to be. Probably this deliberate moderation as we already intimated caused the polemic to be prolonged, for Forner replied in an even more ferocious and hostile manner later on.

In the meantime, however, another writer whose appearance was to have as lasting results as Forner's became involved in the melee. This person was Félix María de Samaniego, the other author of fables who also has been so popular down to our own day. His purpose in writing was different from that of Iriarte since the latter's fables dealt essentially with questions pertaining to literature. Samaniego's were hardly original since they were openly derivative of the works of, among others, Phaedrus and

La Fontaine. They were "moral" fables specifically prepared for
the students of the new *Seminario de Vergara.* The fables were
finished in 1779, and Samaniego sent them to Iriarte for his comments. This action in itself indicates the esteem in which Iriarte
was held at the time. Iriarte's opinion as would be imagined was
favorable, and with this reassuring impetus Samaniego sent them
to press. They first appeared publicly in 1781. Ironically, considering what was to happen, the third book was dedicated to Iriarte:

> In my verses, Iriarte,
> I wish no more art
> Than to have yours as a model.
> To compete I desire
> With your genius, which the learned world admires,
> If you lend me your lyre,
> The one on which played sweetly
> *Music* and *Poetry* jointly.
> (*En mis versos, Iriarte,*
> *Ya no quiero más arte*
> *Que poner á los tuyos por modelo.*
> *Á competir anhelo*
> *Con tu numen, que el sabio mundo admira,*
> *Si me prestas tu lira,*
> *Aquélla en que tocaron dulcemente*
> Música *y* Poesía *juntamente.*) [36]

In spite of all this supposedly good feeling between Samaniego
and Iriarte, when Iriarte's fables appeared some months later
in 1782, Samaniego declared himself on the side of Iriarte's enemies. The reason for this change in attitude must lie in a comment by the editor of Iriarte's fables. The statement is especially
innocent when one considers the inherent difference of purpose
of the two works. The editor writes: "I do not wish to prejudice
the readers' judgment about their merit [of the fables], but only
to note to those least versed in our literature that this is the first
collection of entirely original fables that has been published in
Spanish. And thus as it has for Spain this particular recommendation, it has even another for foreign nations: that is, the novelty
of all its themes being related to literature." [37]

This statement, plus the failure to mention Samaniego's name,
caused the latter's resultant petulance. His reaction is really quite

unacceptable when one considers that Iriarte calls attention to
him specifically in *For Just Such Cases.* In a few lines (in the voice
of Don Eleuterio Geta, the fictitious author) Iriarte states his admiration of Samaniego and also why his own fables are truly
original: "I hold, nevertheless, that just as that able writer to
whom our literature is surely indebted for the first collection of
fables in Spanish verse taken from the best-known fabulists is
your friend Don Félix María de Samaniego, he who in the third
book of his *Moral Fables* praised your poem *Music,* just so the
first person to have *invented* [italics mine] fables in Spanish is
you." [38] It is worth mentioning that Iriarte was a well-known
figure while Samaniego was an unknown—the mere fact that
Samaniego felt obliged to have Iriarte's approval before publishing the fables is indication enough. It is interesting too that
Samaniego was an older man, and age may have been an important psychological factor in his attitude. However unjust we
may consider his petulant childishness, he did proceed to publish
an anonymous pamphlet (without printer or place indicated)
called blatantly enough *Observaciones sobre las Fábulas literarias
originales de D. Tomás de Iriarte (Observations on the "Original"
Literary Fables of Tomás de Iriarte).* The pamphlet was not sold
but was sent to the more renowned members of court society.

This tactic sounds all too much like the devious ways employed before and after by that other more damaging enemy,
Forner. It is sufficient to say that Samaniego, while wanting us
to believe he is an impartial critic, succeeds in condemning the
whole concept of the suitability of the fable to provide rules
concerning the production of literary works. One might ask at this
point how is it that animals are that much better suited to teach
morals—the normal purpose of the fable and of Samaniego's own
collection—than they are to inculcate literary precepts. Samaniego's censure becomes ridiculous if not ludicrous when we carry
his assertions to a logical conclusion. He finally oversteps himself
when he goes on to talk of other works of Iriarte. He calls the
translation of the *Poetics* one of the weakest copies of one of the
most beautiful originals. He assures us that the reply to Sedano is
worthless both in form and content, and almost as an afterthought
he dismisses the poem *Music* as being dated. The specific purpose
of Samaniego then is to prove that Iriarte's talent was not one for
writing fables, that obvious talent of Iriarte which most infuriated

[44]

and wounded Samaniego. The simple truth is that Samaniego wanted no rival. It should be noted here too that much of the antipathy toward Iriarte and the praise of Samaniego that resulted in the nineteenth century and even in our own day came from a biographical sketch of Samaniego done by Eustaquio Fernández de Navarrete. It appeared in an edition (1866) of Samaniego's works. In it he speaks of Iriarte as being the one who satirized Samaniego and says he was jealous of Samaniego and wrote his *Literary Fables* to take away the glory that was Samaniego's. We have already seen the incorrectness of this statement when we noted the dates when Iriarte was working on his poems. This truly unfortunate biography did much damage to Iriarte's stature, a damage that is noted when critics affirm that Iriarte wrote only in anger at Samaniego.[39]

Fortunately Iriarte made no reply to Samaniego in print but he did attempt to have legal action brought against him since the pamphlet had appeared without the necessary license of authority. Nothing came of this action except the discovery of another work by Forner, full of gall as usual, called *Los gramáticos: historia chinesca (The Grammarians: A Chinese History)*. Forner was seeking to have his work published under his real name this time but the Iriartes were successful in keeping it from going to press. Not only was the book a diatribe against Tomás de Iriarte but against the memory of Juan de Iriarte as well. It was a vicious, libelous piece produced by a man who could only have been possessed by a blind, raging envy.

One wonders whether Forner was really not a little warped in his mind at this time. What prompted him to write and to give the above title to his work was Iriarte's having censured some grammatical defects in *The Erudite Ass*. The first "Chinese grammarian" is Juan de Iriarte, whom he accuses of gaining political influence and of then bringing in his nephews to share it (thus we have that same thinly disguised reason for Forner's bitterness). From Chapter Nine on he lunges out at Tomás and Bernardo de Iriarte reiterating the quarrels the youngest brother found himself involved in and sadistically (or masochistically on Forner's part?) telling what happened in each of them. In short, Forner relives all those old polemics while striving to continue a new one. As much as one would like to see the good side of this man, it is very difficult because of his compulsive insistence on being so unlikable. Even when one finds a sentence which is critically incisive, one finds almost always in the next line or two some foolish diatribe that utterly destroys any reason for lending great credence to what he has said in a more sane moment. Even though Fernando Lázaro presents him in a sympathetic tone, the reader comes away shaking his head in disbelief at the nearly paranoid character that is suggested by Forner's words. Such a man would surely make an intriguing subject for a psychological study. Anyone who could scream and jeer as much as did Forner in public against so many prominent people of his day had to be somewhat unbalanced. Although this is a strong statement, one need only look with some care at random selections of his works to come to this conclusion.

When Forner discovered that the Iriarte brothers had sought the assistance of the king in preventing the publication of his book, he wrote to Floridablanca. Some excerpts from the statement of his position very succinctly provide his low opinion of Iriarte: " 'Tomás de Iriarte, a man whose knowledge of letters does not go beyond grammatical studies, but who by having some smattering of the Humanities and some facility in writing verses has come to be persuaded that he is a scholar of the first order and capable of casting his vote in all the sciences. . . .' " [40] Much more in the same vein follows and Forner ends with some laudatory statements to Floridablanca and some self-effacing comments about himself. It is amusing and yet also pathetic to see him doing the same things for which he has damned Iriarte so often. The result of his writing to Floridablanca and his self-praise was completely negative, a result that must have been bitter for him. He did not receive the desired consideration from the Minister although the latter did go so far as to make his opinion of Forner known rather subtly in a short note he added to a document concerning Forner. This note read: " 'And if this young man dedicates himself to serious things and those useful to the public, leaving aside these little impugnments and other similar actions which the French call *des petits auteurs,* I will help him.' " [41]

V *Permanent Establishment of Iriarte*

The appearance of the *Literary Fables* of Tomás de Iriarte definitely established him as the great literary arbiter of his day. In spite of the adverse reactions, reactions that have been dwelt on too much and for too long by critics, Iriarte enjoyed an immediate and resounding popularity. With the publication of this collection of poetry, his dominance of the literary scene, that had been only covertly admitted before, was now hailed from all sides. He was considered from this time forth one of the first, if not the first, authorities in subjects pertaining to letters. From all over Spain he was consulted for his opinions and approval. Such activity was common before but not with the bewildering rapidity that now occurred.

His other works achieved more and more public notice and prominence also. Whenever the *Poetics* of Horace was cited in Spanish translation, for example, it was Iriarte's that was noted. And, as if demanding more of this type of work from him, the public anxiously awaited his translation of the *Aeneid* which he had been working on and which he announced in *For Just Such Cases*. Unfortunately the translation was never completed; Iriarte finished only the first four cantos (see Volume III of the 1787 and 1805 editions). His death ultimately prevented him from completing the translation, but probably a more forceful and singular reason lies in the fear of controversy that Iriarte felt the work might cause when published. When he had translated the *Poetics* he was younger and perhaps more naïve in the ways of critics and his cruelly vindictive enemies. He had not adequately anticipated the controversy that followed the publication of the other translation. A fear of finding himself needlessly and hopelessly embroiled in another quarrel must surely have preyed on his mind. This psychological pressure undoubtedly made him dilatory in his work on the *Aeneid*. The worry about the reception of his book, whether conscious or not, is certainly the main factor in the failure to produce this translation which was so much desired by his friends. Knowing how eager Iriarte was generally for public recognition and approval, it hardly seems correct to believe he never finished the translation because of simple inertia. Certainly this other more profound reason had a much more decisive influence here on his mentality and resulting lack of productivity.

Oddly, when one sees how popular Iriarte had become, one finds that by about 1785 he had begun to lose favor with the Prime Minister, Floridablanca. The arguments of Iriarte's enemies were beginning to produce results, it would seem. Seeking to increase his income and at the same time attempting to get out of the position of Archivist for the Council of War, Iriarte attempted to become Archivist for the Council of State. Since there was no such post, and it was badly needed, he hoped to have one created with himself holding the position. His proposal proved fruitful in one sense: the post was created, but was given to someone else. In addition to this public setback, he found himself in difficulties with the Inquisition. In the last days of Charles III's reign this august body had become more obviously powerful. The complete destruction of Olavide several years earlier is excellent proof that the Inquisition made its strength felt when necessary. Its greatest fear was the invasion of French philosophy which, as the year 1789 approached, became increasingly widespread. As a result of this fear, all Francophiles were suspected of harboring thoughts dangerous to the status quo in Spain. Tomás de Iriarte, as well as his brothers, was certainly among such individuals thought to be too strongly pro-French. It was felt that at best, if he was not anti-Church, he was surely Voltairean or *Encyclopédiste* in spirit.

What started the entire complication of events which ended in Iriarte's censure was very simple—the publication in 1784 of a naïve essay by a Capuchin friar from Pamplona. The *Noticias de cuándo se inventaron las artes (Notices About When the Arts Were Invented)* by Francisco de los Arcos was that type of "informative" book at times very popular in Spain. It and one even more exasperating published in 1786 entitled *Conversaciones instructivas (Instructive Conversations)* belong to that field of imaginative writing that recounts "miracles" and old-wives' tales (it might be added in passing that this genre is surely not singular only to Spain). The Madrid critics had a good time commenting on the tales in the books and the style they exhibited. Most took a serio-comical approach to the works, and as a result many unsuspecting readers, lacking a bit more than ordinary intelligence, accepted them with apparent credulity. Iriarte composed a satirical essay to urge on Fr. Francisco in his efforts; it is called *Carta al R. P. Fr. Francisco de los Arcos, Religioso capuchino, suministrándole ciertas especies para la continuación de su obra intitulada: Conversaciones instructivas (Letter to the Most Reverend Francisco de los Arcos, Capuchin Friar, Providing Him with Certain Examples for the Continuation of His Work En-*

titled: Instructive Conversations). With tongue in cheek for the most part, Iriarte is nevertheless not quite like the other critics because he goes into a very detailed analysis of a similar book published some forty years earlier called *Ilustraciones varias (Various Illustrations)* by a certain Juan Bernardino Rojo. To show exactly what is included in this type of writing Iriarte presents some of the chapter headings that provide such profound information as found in the following: "*Dialogue* XXIV. How many things are necessary in order to be saved. Privileges of the Venetians. When the title of *Infante de España* began. Sterile Women in the Scriptures. The Marys named in them [Scriptures]. And famous women in China. . . ." If Iriarte had stopped here and not interjected some opinions that could hardly be acceptable to a more orthodox mind, he would not have become embroiled with the Inquisition. Among other remarks, he expressed doubts about various characteristics attributed to the Wise Men and about the crossing of the Red Sea by the Hebrews when fleeing from Egypt.[42] These opinions, along with other things which sounded entirely too reminiscent of a Voltairean influence, most likely attracted the attention of the Inquisitors.

In his monumental work on the history of heterodoxy in Spain, Menéndez y Pelayo has some remarks on the inquisitorial suits against Iriarte. He singles out not only Iriarte but Cadalso and Samaniego as well: "There is some doubt that Cadalso was irreligious, but there is none concerning the fabulist Iriarte and his emulator Samaniego; and both aroused the suspicions of the Holy Office. Llorente [see Llorente, *History of the Inquisition of Spain,* pp. 295–96] does not recount their trials very well, either because he did not know much about them or because he wanted to conceal the real motives. He says of Tomás de Iriarte only 'that he was prosecuted by the Inquisition in the last years of the reign of Charles III, as suspected of professing an anti-Christian philosophy; that he was confined to Madrid, with the order to appear when he was summoned; that the proceedings were held in secret; that Iriarte was declared slightly suspect; and that he abjured behind closed doors, only certain penitences being imposed on him.' Tradition adds that he was then exiled to Sanlúcar de Barrameda." Menéndez then goes on to lay full blame for Iriarte's ill luck on one poem. The nineteenth-century critic writes: "Although because of the high positions and the notorious favor that Iriarte and his brother enjoyed in the court the trial was hushed up, there still exists the *corpus delicti,* which is none other than a fable, which after being in manuscript form for so long in the hands of the curious was printed in *El Conciso,* a paper in Cádiz, during the first constitutional period, and from there passed to the *Biblioteca selecta (Select Library)* published by Mendíbil y Silvela in Burdeos in 1819. It is the *oldest heterodox poem that I know in the Spanish language* [italics mine]. It is entitled *La barca de Simón (The Boat of Simon),* that is, that of St. Peter." [43]

The real reason for Iriarte's prosecution was probably a combination of all these factors. Even though Menéndez' statement is extremely significant and singles out Iriarte in a most direct way, it still would seem too easy for this one poem to have almost caused his total downfall. His writings and opinions in general and the tone they gave his name would seem much more likely the cause of his troubles, especially at a time when the Inquisition was analyzing the more outspoken figures of the day to see exactly what their true beliefs were. To lay the blame on one poem alone seems all the more capricious when one finds that during the next year, 1787, Iriarte was complaining bitterly of his persecution. He himself appears uncertain as to precisely what had prompted the actions of the inquisitorial body. He evidently thought that much of the virulent criticism to which he was being inhumanely subjected (witness Forner, for example) was due to his difficulties with the Inquisition. He must have felt this persecution most acutely, for much of his philosophy was unacceptable to that more insulated, isolated aspect of the Spanish mentality of the eighteenth century. That this philosophy undoubtedly had its roots in France was most unfortunate for Iriarte because in the last years of the century that smoldering hatred of the French so long curtailed was beginning to erupt. Iriarte was naturally caught up in the attacks.

An indication of the increasingly more vocal sentiments of the time is the public outcry over an article in the *Encyclopédie Méthodique (Encyclopedia of Method)* by a M. Masson de Morvilliers in which he wrote: "The Spaniard has the aptitude for science; he has a great many books, and nevertheless, his nation is perhaps the most ignorant of Europe. . . . But what does one owe to Spain? And after two centuries, after four, after ten, what has she done for Europe?" [44] Masson was an unknown and would most likely have remained so if Antonio José de Cavanilles, who had been in France for several years, had not taken it upon himself to vindicate the honor of his country. This vindication he undertook by publishing first in France (1784) a pamphlet which was immediately translated into Spanish called simply *Observaciones (Observations)*. He gave a glowing picture of the Spain of his day and in passing mentioned Iriarte quite flatteringly. The essay was well received in France. In Spain, however, it was received with a great uproar and, even more significant, a kind of cathartic outcry against France and her products such as M. Masson. Much was written in defense of the fatherland, and Floridablanca even subsidized a work by Forner, probably his most important, called *Oración apologética por la España (Apologetic Oration For Spain)* and published in 1786. The government subsidy obviously shows that Forner had gained the favor at last of the Prime Minister—at a time when the Iriartes were on a decline in Floridablanca's opinion. Needless to say, the pro-French were not very happy at the favor shown this most mordant enemy. Bernardo de Iriarte, who feared the ultimate break in the union between France and Spain—a union he felt more beneficial to Spain, was most bitter at the whole turn of events:

"This kind of national war broke out tenaciously and ridiculously with Mr. Masson's having composed and printed [his article]. . . . Apologists rained down as a result of that fatal article. The first and principal one of them was Cavanilles, who published his work in Paris in French, and concerning the errors and foolishness it contains as well as the bad results, I formed an extract and critique which I put in the hands of the Count of Floridablanca at his request. Notwithstanding the convincing arguments of this essay which left the Minister confounded and warmly persuaded [to my arguments] . . . he employed the vicious and indiscreet pen of that public defamer Juan Pablo Forner (alias Segarra), so that he might compose, as he did compose, a voluminous, impertinent, and annoying *Apology*, which was printed at royal expense in the Royal Press. . . . In an addition or supplement that Forner put at the end of his *Apology* . . . he committed the beastly mistake of alleging in our favor that if the English presented us with their manufactures and their codfish, they also took from us our wool and other raw materials, without the barbaric apologist reflecting on what was taken from us and what given. . . ." [45]

[51]

Although there is much evidence of Bernardo's jealousy of Forner and his hatred of England, his points are quite sound.

It should be noted that Tomás de Iriarte kept as aloof as possible from this whole polemic. His actions were wise because much of what was written in defense of France or simply in defense of new attitudes was usually only anti-Spanish verbal writhings. What Iriarte did think and say during this time comes down to us in scattered manuscripts and in these he is careful and intelligent: " 'Nothing proves our backwardness so much as the praiseworthy efforts themselves of the government in sending our young people to Paris to study applied mechanics, hydraulics, physics, natural history, mineralogy, and even surgery and anatomy. . . . In the mechanical arts we know nothing. The good patriot will not be the one who declaims, but who works; the one who writes one of the infinite books we need. Speaking only of letters, we do not have a good Spanish grammar, an epic poem, a study of synonyms, a study of matrices, etc., etc. In regard to industry and commerce, when the shirt we put on is ours, when such precious raw materials like wool do not leave the country, when, etc., then we can boast. God grant that it be soon! As long as this does not happen, all apologies are unfounded and sophistic; and they will be useless.' " [46]

Iriarte in what he says here indicates better than ever that sense of proportion and measure that was always his. He sounds like his brother but with a great deal less compulsion and anger. There is no outward condemnation of the state of the nation, but there is indeed a profound sadness that a true lover of his homeland would feel on seeing the state of affairs at that time. Granted, some of Iriarte's despair was due to personal reasons, but he should not be relegated to the camp of backbiters where some later critics have attempted to put him. It is only natural that he would feel a certain disenchantment with the present state of affairs wherein he was being maligned from several sides. On one of these sides was Forner who was beginning to find himself in increasing favor with the ruling party while Iriarte's position was no longer so favorable as it had been formerly. That Iriarte managed to deliver his thoughts in such tempered language as that quoted above is greatly to his credit. A less reasonable person would surely have chosen this time of national confusion to deliver his thoughts in a self-righteous, pious, smug manner. Iriarte says in the simplest way possible what he sees as the plight of his country. And interestingly he has been borne out in the course of time since his death. To see the true caliber of his personality, this passage is invaluable.

As we have seen in previous cases, the sentiments of Tomás de Iriarte at this time too were those of his brothers as well. Domingo by now had become Secretary to the Spanish embassy in France, which was headed by the former Prime Minister, the Count of Aranda. Aranda was very anxious to become Prime Minister once again, and since he had always been a friend of the Iriarte brothers, they naturally tended to align themselves with his political faction. Any difficulties such an alignment might produce were of little consequence, for evidently by this time they felt themselves irreparably estranged from Floridablanca. In itself such action by the Iriartes was not unexpected. It was perhaps less fortunate for them, from a political standpoint only, that Tomás decided to publish more and more of his work. For once he failed to use adequately his political sagacity. At this rather unpropitious time for a decent reception, his works were made public with increased frequency. Some of them appeared separately in journals of the day. Most important for Iriarte and his later readers, however, was the first edition of his complete works which came out in 1787.[17]

The same thing now happened that had occurred at the publications of his earlier works. Iriarte's new venture was met with both loud acclaim and vituperation. The fact that he would have the audacity to publish all his works was heresy to his detractors. They leaped upon their archenemy as if starving for a feast. Again it is so intriguing to note the nearly maniacal manner of Iriarte's decriers. Their own lack of accomplishment and their omission from the society whose association they coveted so much are more than likely the basic reasons for their morbidity, and not Iriarte himself or his work. About 1787 we have then the convergence of three events in Iriarte's career, all of which greatly influenced the last days of his life: the loss of Floridablanca's assistance, the Masson article and the hysterical chauvinism it caused in Spain placing Iriarte in an awkward position because of his somewhat pro-French attitudes, and the publication of Iriarte's works which brought about the renewal of the particularly bitter and unhappy polemic with Samaniego. In the first two situations Iriarte had done nothing to provoke an outcry against himself. In the renewed arguments with Samaniego the fault again was not Iriarte's. Throughout all these unpleasant events Iriarte maintained a discreet silence and distance, trying not to awaken any unnecessary animosity. It is completely just therefore to lay the blame for the new polemic at Samaniego's feet. Samaniego, bitter now at his total eclipse by Iriarte, was determined to cry out against the younger poet no matter how weak his own position in such a confrontation might be. In addition to some verses he composed, he wrote a *Carta apologética al señor Masson (An Apologetic Letter to Mr. Masson)* which is essentially an ironic, sarcastic diatribe against Iriarte using the Masson crisis as a good occasion for advancing his own ends. Such an attitude was far different from Iriarte's.

While all this public bickering was going on, Iriarte returned to composing plays. He was caught up in a resurgence of general interest in the drama that had been growing for some time. This interest in a new direction was also to blame for some of the criticism leveled at him in these years, for his enemies did not want to see him gaining more popularity in a field that would unquestionably keep his name before the public. We saw earlier how he had translated and written plays in the 1770's. He had never totally disregarded his desire for composing drama; he had merely given himself to other literary genres where he thought his talents could be more useful. He was always eager to reform; this characteristic has been seen repeatedly in the works noted so far. It was undoubtedly with the idea of reforming once and for all the antiquated Spanish drama that he now took up where he had left off some years earlier.

By the end of the 1780's the smoldering jealousy and rancor between the pro- and anti-French cliques definitely began to reach a peak. Those who would have sought to uphold the Spanish genius while not totally rejecting the advantages of certain French innovations satisfied neither side and were attacked roundly by both. It was precisely this blind rage that overwhelmed the laudable efforts of Vicente García de la Huerta. In 1785 he published his *Theatro hespañol (Spanish Theater)* with which he hoped to restore his country's drama to a position of critical, as well as popular, acceptance. He was immediately embroiled in a most bitter polemic, finding himself attacked from both sides, each venting its own spleen on an innocent victim. The pro-French criticized him for even attempting to endorse certain native works. To these more "reasonable" men the wild flight from the unities and the complete lack of proportion in the national theater caused it to seem barbaric and without any merit whatever. The anti-French criticized him for attempting to find a certain sense of proportion and moral tone in this theater. Obviously the balanced critic could never bring together two such diametrically opposed groups, each becoming constantly shriller in its protests. Huerta's *Theater* had tremendous value certainly, but due to the blindness of the enraged critics of the time little praise was given to the author in appreciation for his efforts. Whether the battle was a direct cause or not, Huerta died in the midst of it in 1787.

It is generally believed that Iriarte remained aloof during this whole disgraceful episode although there are those who believe he was the author of a *Carta (Letter)*, 1787, that is not too laudatory of Huerta's intentions. It is not at all certain, however, who the author was. At any rate, whatever his public utterances were, by 1788 Iriarte had definitely become the spokesman or leader for the pro-French point of view regarding Spanish drama. To show his powerful position and undoubtedly to awe his enemies, he ventured determinedly into the field of drama on his own with a play entitled *El señorito mimado (The Pampered Youth)*. The none-too-happy reception of *The Busybody* several years earlier had made him more careful in choosing his subject—always a moralistic one. This time he turned to the field of contemporary education. Still remembering previous difficulties, rather than subject his play and himself first to a too vocally exuberant public, he took advantage of the publication of his complete works and had *The Pampered Youth* included in the fourth volume. He hoped in this way to allow the work to avoid a confrontation with a rowdy audience. It was his intention to have it presented on the stage if it received favorable acclaim from his readers. One example of the response it occasioned is enough to see why Iriarte was able to go ahead at once with his plans for producing the play:

"Don Tomás de Iriarte (as he is one of those who carry the banner of good taste) has rejected for his part a similar objection [that dis-

cussing plays was not the same thing as writing them], publishing this
original play, in which not only do I not find any defect, but, if needs
be, I would challenge any critic and even the most envious man to
point out to me a single error in it. This well-known and fine talent
can compete in the theater with the most outstanding of all Europe,
since we see in this delightful work a truly comic style . . . a great
deal of charm and wit not of that type which only pleases those who
go to the theater to eat oranges . . . fluent diction . . . witty sayings,
and all done in such a way as not to seem recherché but born naturally
from the situations themselves in the drama. . . . Not only does it
merit a license so it can be presented, but it would be wise to thank
the author so that, in view of this example of honor and distinction,
other talented writers might be stimulated to imitate him, thus presenting new dramas, which is the best way of emending and correcting
our theater." [48]

With such an enthusiastic endorsement, it is natural to assume
the play would be a success when produced, and such was the
case at its premiere on September 9, 1788. There were those who
sought to annoy the author by indirectly slighting him, praising
only the actors and attributing the success of the play to them
and not to the playwright. Forner, who was jealous of this new
popularity of Iriarte, followed this same line of thought in a
letter written to a friend, Eugenio Llaguno. The letter was never
published. In general, however, the criticism was favorable.

Not content with censuring the education provided for young
men, Iriarte felt that for young women also needed exposure to
criticism. It was with this intent that he began writing *La señorita
mal-criada* (*The Ill-Bred Miss*) which was finished shortly after the
publication of *The Pampered Youth*. The new play was published
in 1788. The critics were as kind with this play as they had been
with the previous one. A typical comment is this one taken from
La Espigadera, a weekly paper of the day (for which critics like
Forner often wrote): " 'One wishes that in our theater many plays
so well arranged and worthy of praise as is this one might be
presented, and that those who provide the stage with farces
would dedicate themselves to study nature more and to follow
the proper road of regularity and good taste where the present
author has known how to conduct himself. . . .' " [49] For some reason
the success of this play on the stage was not what its initial
reception with its readers would have indicated. It was not

produced until January 3, 1791. Even though it lasted for a week
(which was not bad, considering that even the best-received
plays often did not last longer), it was rated a poor success. Since
the reaction of the critics was favorable on its publication in
1788, it does not seem proper to lay the blame for its failure on
Iriarte. Indeed, the critics of the day thought that the actors
killed the play. In the papers of the time there are various references in verse to what happened. They all are unanimous in their
dislike of the actors' performances. In this instance it was fortunate
the initial appearance of the work was not on the stage, for
otherwise its true merits might have been irreparably damaged
by an inadequate presentation.

VI Death of Iriarte

From 1788 on we find a kind of withdrawal into himself on
the part of Iriarte. It was as if he were tired of the unceasing
attacks and inevitable polemics that grew up around him. Even
when there was good news such as the generally approving reception given the works mentioned above, Iriarte himself was suffering more acutely from his perennial physical ailment, gout. This
disease made it all the more difficult for him to court society
willingly. And with what was occurring in society, it is no great
wonder that he began quietly to retire somewhat from that life
he had hitherto so much enjoyed.

The society of the capital was in a state of flux. The national
government was undergoing profound changes with the death
of Charles III and the ascension of his inept son, Charles IV. In
addition there were concerted efforts to remove the one able
leader still in power, the Count of Floridablanca. Evidently sens-
ing a certain portending doom in the atmosphere, Iriarte began
to devote his days to projects which he would not always complete but which were so much a part of his convictions as a
writer—to teach and thereby to elevate society's moral behavior.
The two most significant projects were directed at Spanish youth
and fortunately were published. One was the *Lecciones instructivas sobre la historia y la geografía (Instructive Lessons on History and Geography)*, which appeared in 1791 after the author's
death. It was to go through many successive editions and, in its
day, was very much needed as a clear, simple presentation of
facts that all too often were generally unknown. Pignatelli pro-

vides us an interesting comment on this work and its fate. In it
we again see the importance Bernardo de Iriarte had in the
publishing of much of his brother's work: "Different circumstances
and some unpleasantness which were caused him [Tomás de
Iriarte] when he tried to have his *Lessons* printed were the cause
of this printing being suspended; and he died leaving [the work]
unedited and with the idea of publishing it some day on his own
with those additions and improvements which seemed wise to
him. We owe to the zeal of his brother Bernardo Yriarte, [he who
was] so interested in his glory, that [the work] has since been
presented to the public, from which it has merited the most
complete approbation." [50]

The other book was a translation of the German writer Campe's
*El nuevo Robinsón, historia moral, reducida a diálogos para in-
strucción y entretenimiento de niños y jóvenes de ambos sexos,
escrita recientemente en alemán, por el señor Campe, traducida
al inglés, al italiano, al francés y de éste al castellano con varias
correcciones por D. Tomás de Iriarte* (*The New Robinson, A
Moral History, Reduced to Dialogues for the Instruction and
Entertainment of Children and Youth of Both Sexes, Written Recently in German by Mr. Campe and Translated into English,
Italian, French and from the Latter into Spanish with Various
Emendations by Tomás de Iriarte*). It came out in 1789 in two
volumes and contained several fine plates to illustrate better the
places mentioned in the work. It too had numerous editions.

As his health continued about the same with little or no im-
provement, Iriarte at last decided to go to the South of Spain
where he hoped he would at least be more comfortable. He spent
most of the year 1790 in the port town Sanlúcar de Barrameda.
It will be remembered that Menéndez y Pelayo points out the tradition that Iriarte retired here because the Inquisition forced him
to do so. This is entirely without foundation. He maintained an active correspondence with his friends in Madrid so as not to lose
completely the invigorating atmosphere that that city provided
and that he so avidly desired. One of those to whom he wrote
most often was the Duchess of Osuna for whom he composed
while in Sanclúcar the play entitled *El don de gentes* (*Winning
Ways*) which was not printed until some time after his death. In
this play his intention was to present the perfect type of woman—
intelligent, pleasant, and discreet. It is significant that he should

[58]

dedicate such a play to the one woman whom he very much admired and who had helped him in various ways.[51] He also wrote for her a short piece called *Donde menos se piensa salta la liebre (It Would Happen Where Least Expected)*. In the production of both these plays the Duchess took an active part, seeing to it that they were presented in accordance with the author's intentions.

When Iriarte found little relief from his illness, he returned to Madrid. He did obtain some respite for a short while here and during this time he was able to see two of his works produced with great success, a success which undoubtedly made up for the unsatisfactory acceptance some weeks earlier of *The Ill-Bred Miss*. Between February 15 and 26 of 1791, *The Pampered Youth* was presented by an entire company of women, and on February 26 a new work was given with much immediate acclaim. This was his *melólogo* (melologue) *Guzmán el bueno (Guzmán, The Good)*, written while Iriarte was in Sanclúcar. As usual Iriarte's enemies were eager in their negative criticisms, even before the favorable popular opinion could really make itself heard. Among the most vociferous of these critics was Samaniego, who saw still another chance to slight the man whom he had unsuccessfully tried to slander several years before. He now composed a type of parody in which he followed Iriarte's *Guzmán* very closely. The whole business sounds childish and hardly worthy of a supposedly intelligent man. The only reason he did not publish what he wrote was the death of Iriarte.

Iriarte's illness became worse in the spring of 1791. In the summer he was bedridden almost constantly. What made his suffering even worse was that at times he would experience a sudden, but short, relief which would restore his hopes of recovery, hopes that would then be rudely dashed. Pignatelli offers some insight into what the disease was like and how it had affected the writer all along: ". . . the illness of gout . . . very soon began to overcome him and conducted him to the grave. He had consulted several learned doctors about this disease; he had read everything that had been written about gout and had subjected himself more than once to the most rigorous diet, suspending his literary tasks in order to see whether in that way he could temper the harshness of the disease. But all was in vain." [52]

In his last days Iriarte was nevertheless able to maintain a cheerful posture in the presence of his friends, but this gaiety covered a rather bitter interior. Again we turn to Pignatelli for an intimate description of what he was like in the last few days of his life:

It is said of some people that they were able to keep their inherent good humor when at the very doors of death, but few of them have been able to keep their sense of humor in the midst of the most acute pain. Of this truth those of us who witnessed his very last moments can give testimony. How many times did he himself on seeing our emotion console us with maxims of true philosophy and with such ingenious reflections proper to a personality so clear and free as his own. . . . Finally, after having complied with all the obligations of a Christian, this renowned writer died on September 17, 1791. During this last illness he had composed three fables, one of which painted the uncertainty of the art of medicine. A few days before his death he dictated to one of his attendants a sonnet in which he said how little a success in the career of letters was conducive to happiness.[53]

This particular sonnet is a melancholy testimonial to Tomás de Iriarte's life and to his attitude in his last years. There is no self-pity by any means but rather a realistic, almost cynical acceptance of what a literary career, to him his very life, really was. The writer himself is restrained, although admittedly he is bitter when he refers directly to Forner in the sonnet's last line. It is somehow fitting to think of Tomás de Iriarte in his last moments dictating a poem in which he maintains that sadly stoic attitude exhibited throughout his life.

CHAPTER 2

La poética, Donde las dan las toman, and *La música*

I La poética (Poetics) *of Horace*

IN the preceding chapter where the life of Tomás de Iriarte was briefly sketched, the works that comprised the greatest portion of his literary endeavors were mentioned in relation to the significant events of his career. Some of these works caused certain occurrences in his life and determined in what directions the writer himself would move. Such was the case with his translation of Horace's *Poética (Poetics* or *Letter to the Pisones).* Obviously the work is not an original one, but in Iriarte's vision of Horace's work, in his treatment of the ideas, and in his unusual means of explaining events in the poem he does make the work to a great extent his own. It was because of these very same reasons that he was criticized vehemently by his enemies. These criticisms in turn dictated Iriarte's reactions and thus the course of events in the immediately ensuing years. The *Poetics* therefore is the first work of Iriarte that truly stamps the development of his character in any way. It is not the first of his productions, since he had written previously, nor is it the most important of his works. However, it appears when he is twenty-seven (1777) and just as he is beginning to find his directions as a writer. And what is more important is that it is the first major production showing his philosophy both as a writer and as a man of his time. 1777 also marks the beginning of his period of greatest literary activity and fecundity, for in 1780 *La música (Music)* appears and in 1782, his *Fábulas literarias (Literary Fables).* By starting *in medias res,* as it were, we can look back and see where he was going prior to this time and look ahead to see where his ideas would lead him.

The *Poetics,* although we must say again it is a translation, is important for another reason—the work itself embodies those precepts Iriarte believed most binding for every writer. The desire

[61]

to polish, to select, to restrain is inherent in Iriarte from his first declarations on the subject of writing. Most certainly the basis for these ideas comes from his early study of the Classical writers, specifically Horace. To understand Iriarte and his concept of literary production is to understand the Classical mind regarding the same subject. By seeing Horace's work here presented in the Spanish language with Iriarte's own stamp, we shall begin to comprehend not only the development of Iriarte's career but his significance in and effect on the times in which he lived. In the short discussion about this work in Chapter 1, it was noted that Iriarte himself made a definitive statement about his love and veneration for the Roman poet. He says Horace is his library in which he finds pleasure, assistance, and interestingly a realization that his own creative powers are limited in comparison. From his early study of Latin he knew Horace profoundly by the time he set out on his project of translating, for a few lines further on in this same poem he states that Horace has always been the supreme judge for him. There has never been any ". . . passion, error or caprice/ Nor does anything happen/ That I do not find some judgment" in Horace whether it concern the fatuous orator, the envious intellectual, the superstitious fool or any of those ". . . others who in society/ Are such bothersome individuals. . . ." [1] In other words, Horace becomes a kind of deity for Iriarte.

The translation of the *Poetics* was done in a relatively short time. Iriarte states in a letter to Cadalso in October, 1777, that he did the work in the leisure hours of a vacation.[2] He undertook this project as a labor of love, not as a commercial venture. The letter makes its point quite clear because Iriarte is scolding Cadalso lightly for not having responded to his dedication of the book to him, an old friend. He asserts that if he had wanted to win the patronage of someone more financially stable he could easily have done so. He says his purpose was rather to honor a friend who esteemed Horace as much as he. He goes on to say that he translated while he was at ease from the ordinary cares of a daily routine, while he could become totally involved in the work and spirit of the writer who molded his thinking more than anyone else. To write with no other cares was his way of communicating with, and of totally imbibing, the spirit of his mentor. Thus, again we see the value of this translation, not necessarily so much from a visible, physical standpoint this time but from a mental and emotional stance at the source for most of his own ideas and precepts.

Although he wrote the translation in a short time, Iriarte had first spent much time in studying this work and other translations and studies of it.[3] He was moved to undertake the translation because of the inadequate versions of the poem already in Spanish. He is quite candid about his own limitations for such an undertaking but feels so deeply about the situation that he must present his offering to the public. In his introduction to the translation he writes:

The importance of the version of that *Epistle* in the Spanish language and verse incited me to undertake this project; although the great difficulty of penetrating well the sense of the original and of expressing the force of it with intelligible verses . . . , should have dissuaded me from the attempt. The consideration that we already have in our language some translations of this work in verse might also have dissuaded me from my purpose; the principal and best known translations being those written in different times by Vicente Espinel and the Catalan Jesuit Joseph Morell. But the careful examination of both confirmed me even more in the idea that we still needed to know Horace better.[4]

To undertake the task of translating such a well-known work involved a great deal of courage on Iriarte's part. The difficulty of the work itself, which he readily admitted, was enough to deter any ordinary translator. In addition to this more apparent difficulty there was the very real possibility of arousing negative criticism from many different quarters. It was this fear, a fear that was to haunt him at the writing of every work afterward, that was uppermost in his mind. There were conceivably many occasions to arouse such criticism. Were he to be careless in translating at any point he would be certain to provoke censure. Were he to misinterpret or simply to interpret passages differently from the accepted versions he would be apt to invite reprimands. But any translator knows these pitfalls and if he is truly a conscientious scholar, he assiduously avoids them. The possibility of his enemies' condemning his work for no other reason than jealousy and spite was what really worried Iriarte. In several letters now in the National Library in manuscript form he plainly shows he was seeking to avoid any unnecessary censure. And when the translation appeared in 1777 he found he was nevertheless unreasonably maligned in many instances. In rebuttal he wrote a *Carta familiar y apologética en satisfacción a varios reparos sobre la nueva traducción del Arte poética de Horacio (Familiar and Apologetic Letter to Satisfy Several Criticisms Concerning the New Translation of the Poetics of Horace).* Supposedly it was directed to his friends, but it is really against those who only cry out against anything done by a more adventuresome, productive person than themselves. As was to be the case with all his works, the hue and cry for and against him reached such proportions that the real value of his efforts later became diminished or at least was not fully appreciated.

What caused the most uproar and the unhappy results for both Iriarte and his critic was the discussion Iriarte wrote in his preliminary dialogue concerning the Espinel translation of the *Poetics.* He states that this translation and the one by the Catalan Jesuit Joseph Morell received much more acclaim than they deserved. He reserves most of his condemnation for Espinel's work and criticizes it only because he believes the public needs to be undeceived about its relative lack of worth. He presents a number of reasons for his censure of the translation so as to show the honesty of his intentions and also so as to provide a solid foundation for what he writes. He mentions on pages iv and v of this introductory material that the Espinel translation is to be found in the first volume (published in 1768) of a collection of Spanish poetry called the *Parnaso español (Spanish Parnassus).* Later on he becomes more specific in his criticism and can see no good reason for the Espinel translation's being included in a collection such as this is, one in which only the best works of Spanish writers were to be included:

After this quick sketch, to which I do not dare to give the title of a formal and complete critique, but which is enough to show the carelessness in the translation by Vicente Espinel, it is not easy for me to pay no attention to the exaggerated praise that is given to it in the first volume of the *Spanish Parnassus.* There it is called "perfect, excellent, and happily adapted to its original"; one is assured there is nothing in it "superfluous or voluntarily inserted"; that "in its free verse the vigor and natural grace of the original are preserved, acquiring new strength and spirit with the Spanish sentence"; and finally, that "the versification is full, fluid and sonorous." [5]

He also censures Morell but not so unfavorably as he does Espinel: "[Morell's translation] has much the advantage over Vicente Espinel's because that translator generally understood better than [Espinel] the true sense of many of Horace's precepts; because he is more ingenious in his Spanish verses . . . or because finally he explains with opportune notes several obscure passages of the original." [6]

To show how he has benefitted from the errors that he enumerates in the translators' works, he explains why he has diverged from their directions or else chosen to emulate them in their good points. In one place he notes that his translation is longer than the original (1065 verses as compared to the original 477). He fails to understand how the editor of the *Spanish Parnassus* (Juan José López de Sedano) could criticize Espinel for the lack of brevity when he, Iriarte, believes this is one of Espinel's good points since, though he writes more verses, he is better able to capture the essence of the inherently more concise Latin verses of Horace. He is surprised too that the editor wrote his criticism in Volume III of his collection.[7] From here he goes on to state that the style of his own translation too is more verbose than Horace's, but he reasons that the Spanish tongue is of necessity more verbose than the Latin. He realizes he has made himself the ideal target for critics and tries to clarify his method of translating by illustrating it here in the introduction:

. . . [and] so as to resolve some difficulties that occur in the context of the translation itself, at times I have not hesitated to use two entire verses to explain only one or two words of Horace. Thus when translating in verse 471 these two words *triste bidental,* although I could put like the Jesuit Morell *triste bidental* and then explain in a note that the *bidental* was the sign that the Ancients put at the place where a thunderbolt had fallen, I prefer to translate in this way: "The sign that denotes as sacred/The sad place where fell a flash of lightning." To give greater clarity and force to the expression, I frequently add some epithets, conjunctions, adverbs, etc., to the original; but I try not to invent them capriciously but to take them, if possible, from the idea itself of the author following his thinking and his style . . . neither would it be possible to make a translation verse by verse unless these means were justified for the translator who takes advantage of them opportunely and moderately. And if because of the necessity of using this license in places in which the meter requires it or because of the desire to elucidate the concepts of Horace, adapting them to the spirit of our language, it is noted that sometimes my translation is extended more than the original requires, at other times it will be noted that I have succeeded in accommodating a Latin verse . . . [of thirteen to sixteen syllables] into one in Spanish that has only eleven.[8]

Iriarte ends his introduction to the *Poetics* on a quite humble and candid note. He points out the value of the Latin work and the difficulty of even approaching the original. The real values of the *Poetics* are underlined once and for all. They are those values that guided Iriarte throughout his entire literary career. They serve to impress upon our minds what Iriarte was always seeking in everything he wrote—to entertain but above all to teach: "Concerning the first circumstance in which Horace observes that good writers must provide something useful and instructive, I have the satisfaction of having chosen a work from among the most useful and instructive which are known in literature; but concerning the second requirement which is pleasantness and delight I shall not dare to boast equally of having achieved success; since with some confusion on my part I have discovered, on transposing this *Epistle* into our language, the great distance between Latin and Spanish poetry, and the great distance between Horace and his translator."[9]

Iriarte's translation of the *Poetics* occupies some sixty-six pages in the 1787 edition of his works, excluding the long prologue and extensive notes at the end. He has placed the Latin original at the bottom of each page. Iriarte's verse form is the *silva*, a form long used by the most renowned Spanish writers, so he informs us in the prologue. He has preferred this type of verse because with its liberty in rhyme and in the combination of seven- and eleven-syllabic lines he has been able to achieve a harmony and naturalness impossible in more rigorous meters.[10]

The work itself was originally written as a letter to some friends of Horace to serve as a guide for writing. In addition, exhortations to follow the dictates of prudence, circumspection, and naturalness are found regarding all aspects of life. The Horatian poem has come down to us as a compendium of proper taste to be demanded in all the arts. Such admonitions as to observe the people around us and their customs so as to understand better the ways of man in his different ages and the world he lives in seem almost commonplace to us now.[11] The idea that Nature is the model for all human endeavors and must be imitated to achieve a truly real balance in life or in our works is still another long-accepted cardinal precept.[12] Probably Horace's best-known mandate is that the author who truly wishes to be great and to be worthwhile at the same time is he who writes not only with the intention of giving pleasure but of instructing or teaching as well. The concept of *utile dulci* [13] has its real basis here and, as noted in Chapter 1 of the present study, it is that concept so basic to all serious literary production in the eighteenth century.

These few examples give some idea as to what Horace's work is like. What is of more interest to us is how the precepts included in his poem affect Iriarte's own writing. There are instances where the influence is openly apparent. The most notable of these has to do with Iriarte's method of translating. He explains in notes much of what would not be readily clear to the ordinary reader. This scheme is natural for any translator and commentator. However, Iriarte goes beyond this purely encyclopedic approach and incorporates his explanations into the text itself, a characteristic that offended his more vitriolic critics. This habit is another reason too for the extra length of his translation. What Iriarte's critics rather foolishly overlooked is that Horace himself indirectly gives permission for such license. Early in this very poem Horace admonishes a writer to choose his ideas well and to know how to discard thoughts that are not always relevant. From there he goes on to talk about introducing new words into the language if there is no adequate way of getting the idea across in the already existing language—as long as one is prudent in his new vocabulary, he is completely within his rights to write as he pleases. Within this very section Iriarte adds some words that explain Horace's intentions without the necessity of any notes. In his preliminary discourse he explains what he has done:

I have tried to clarify the meaning of many intricate verses of the original by adding some words, avoiding in this way (when it has been possible) some lengthy notes which would be necessary in order to decipher all that Horace was trying to say. Verses 63, 64, and others up to 68 of the original text serve as examples. Horace, in order to support his idea that nothing that men do is lasting, says literally in those lines: "Whether Neptune received on the land defends the squadron from the North winds (the work of a king); or whether the lake, sterile for a long time and suitable for boats, maintains neighboring cities and feels the heavy plowshare; or whether the River, taught to follow a better course, has changed its course harmful to the grain fields." *Neptune received on land* alludes to the undertaking of Julius Caesar, continued by Augustus, of opening the *Julian Port*, cutting through the land between the sea and the Lakes of Lucrino and Averno. The *sterile lake*, etc., alludes to the *Pontine Lake* which Augustus himself ordered drained so that it could later be useful land. And the *River which changed its course* alludes to the work which this same emperor had done in order to contain the floods of the Tiber. All this would be confusing if one were to translate the original literally; and it only could be understood through a long commentary.[14]

The internal quotation above is in the text later where he has incorporated *Julian Port, Pontine Lake,* and a description of what was done to the Tiber into the translation itself. Iriarte has thus not only made the reading more easily understandable, but ingeniously he has followed Horace's precept within the framework of the precept itself. This characteristic of Iriarte's manner of translating was repudiated by some critics and may even have given rise to some of the strictures that Cotarelo rarely delivers wherein he condemns the length and redundancy of the translation.[15] Nevertheless, Iriarte has captured the essence of Horace's dictates and proceeds to show how well he has grasped them in a most convincing manner.

II Donde las dan las toman (Give and Take)

Whatever the critics said about his translation of Horace's *Poetics,* the one thing Iriarte did wrong was to question the reasons for including the Espinel translation in the *Spanish Parnassus.* Earlier in this chapter Iriarte's specific criticisms of the Espinel work were quoted. He was most disturbed that a poorly executed work should be praised so highly by its editor—in this case, Sedano. The translation was neither a good example of Spanish poetry nor a credit to Espinel himself, who should have been remembered for other, more fortunate endeavors. Had Iriarte not censured the unmerited praise given so freely in Volume I and qualified somewhat in Volume III of the *Spanish Parnassus,* he would never have become involved in the first really

extensive polemic of his literary career. The editor Sedano reacted to Iriarte's statements as if they had been directed at him
personally and replied in Volume IX of the *Parnassus* (1778) to
Iriarte's criticisms in an almost vicious way.

The most acceptable explanation for Sedano's behavior is a
psychological one. Sedano had praised the Espinel translation
rather unintelligently in the first volume but then, being criticized
by his peers, he attempted to retract in Volume III some of his
previous enthusiasm. He naturally as an editor and critic was in
a most unhappy and vulnerable position. When Iriarte criticized
his judgments for being precisely so unwarranted and vacillating,
he obviously hit the core of Sedano's weakness, and the latter
lashed back at the most visible object, which turned out to be
Iriarte's work and Iriarte himself. He was unable to reply properly
to Iriarte and as a result generalized about Iriarte's so-called errors in interpretation, without quoting any, and even tried to
malign Iriarte's name. All of what he had to say put him in a
more untenable position. His petulance only got him into more
trouble, for Iriarte replied in one of the best-developed critical
dialogues of the period. It is called *Donde las dan las toman
(Give and Take).* It was first published in the heat of the argument
in 1778 and was later included in the first edition of the author's
complete works. In his introduction to the sixth volume of this
collection he states his reasons for reproducing a work that has
already involved "a question in which both [Sedano and Iriarte]
have expressed their arguments too extensively." But previous to
this sentence he does state what the basic values of this work of
criticism are:

The critical essays which compose the sixth and last volume would
not be therefore in this collection if the curious, who still deign to
look for and read them, were to find in them only a personal defense
of the author or an outlet for their own literary resentments. This
matters little indeed to the public. But if it is true that in said essays
. . . there are notices and observations which can provide some fruit,
then this is a basic motive for reprinting them. In the jocular-serious
dialogue entitled *Give and Take* the meaning of various difficult passages of the *Epistle* of Horace to the Pisones is explained, the worth of
some Spanish poems inserted in the collection of the *Spanish Parnassus*
is examined, and many errors concerning the lives of our different

poets are noted. This can lead to the good of literature and for this reason alone it is published. . . .[16]

The dialogue is carried on by three personages: Don Justo, who is a kind of mediator, Don Cándido, who is Sedano's representative, and the Translator, who is of course Iriarte. The treatment of all points of view is in general quite fair and the men speak in reasonable, moderate language. Iriarte accepts the criticisms handed out by Cándido and then refutes the statements or explains more fully what he meant. In the beginning, while defending his prologue and the position taken therein, he affirms that he certainly was not the first to speak negatively of Espinel's translation. His uncle is quoted as having said: "Poor Horace in the hands of poor Espinel!" [17] He then points out that Sedano has said the very same things about the Espinel translation as he himself did and he therefore sees no excuse for Sedano to criticize him now. In fact, the only difference he can find is that his own critique is longer than Sedano's and perhaps Sedano is jealous of that fact. Iriarte also wants to know how, if Sedano himself called the translation improper, can he possibly have defended it and much less reasonably put it in the first volume of his collection. In this particular part of the dialogue he notes the confusion and contradictions that Sedano has obviously gotten himself into.[18] Iriarte then throws back at Cándido Sedano's criticism of his verbosity when he asks whether a good critic is simply to condemn a work without giving specific reasons for doing so. He becomes rather sarcastic and humorous when he rephrases Sedano's words: ". . . but I, although I pass for *intrepid*, have not had the intrepidity to assure that in Espinel there are *improprieties* without providing a few examples like those I have noted." [19]

From here he goes on to discuss the errors in Espinel's translation more at length since this is what Sedano has demanded of him. He reemphasizes that his intention was never to criticize an author whom he really very much admires. He repeats his contention that it is extremely unfortunate that this particular work of Espinel should have been chosen to head a collection that was to have included the best of Spanish writing. As far as Espinel's value as a writer is concerned, he has only praise for him. Iriarte continues his defense by saying that his criticisms

La poética, Donde las dan las toman, and *La música*
were never personal since the first five volumes of the *Parnassus*
appeared without the editor's name and no one need really have
known that it was Sedano. In his own remarks in his translation
of Horace, he never mentioned anyone by name. He only said
that in such and such a volume certain inaccuracies could be
found. He points out that it is really the editor who has brought
upon himself all this public censure at the present time: "[Iriarte]
publishing his translation of the *Poetics* with his given name, surname, and position, spoke of an anonymous work [the *Parnassus*];
and the editor comes forth now . . . unmasked to vindicate the
offense which was not made against his person: which is the same
as to say that the matter is to be treated as a personal and direct
one from Juan López Sedano against Tomás de Iriarte, when it
might have remained a mere literary altercation of book against
book." [20]

In response to Sedano's contention that Iriarte criticized other
translations to praise his own indirectly, Iriarte vehemently states
that such was never his intention and that no expression of praise
of his own work is to be found anywhere in his translation. He
even is somewhat self-effacing (as was noted in the preliminary
material to the translation itself), admitting that it was extremely
difficult to penetrate the sense of the original work, a task that
he fears he may not have succeeded in as well as he would have
liked.[21] He somewhat turns the tables by endeavoring to show
Sedano's lack of education and his obvious provincialism by
employing certain words the editor himself used. He does prove
Sedano to be rather inept in the choice of his vocabulary. His
criticisms also demonstrate that Iriarte is a purist when it comes
to the makeup and function of language. This undoubtedly is a
result of his early training in the Classical languages under the
tutelage of his uncle. Iriarte continues in this same vein of ridicul-
ing Sedano by launching into an attack on a play *(Jahel)* by the
editor that was written in the 1760's. He succeeds in criticizing
Sedano in the very same words the latter used when talking
about Iriarte's translation of the *Poetics*—i.e., it is too extensive,
diffuse, and redundant. Since his remarks have now taken on
a more personal tone, Iriarte launches into a critique of the
Parnassus in general. He says that as a collection it can only be
described by the monstrous figure Horace painted at the beginning of his *Poetics*—its head is didactic, its neck lyrical, and its

other parts composed of the satiric, the epic, the dramatic, and the bucolic. In short, it is an abominable creation that should never have been let loose. Not only is the work such an ungainly hybrid; it is filled with inaccuracies in the biographical and historical material it contains. To substantiate his contention, Iriarte provides a list of such errors.[22] He sums up his findings in a comprehensive way:

Let us conclude, then, so as not to talk any more about the *Spanish Parnassus* that that work as has been shown has no method to it; that in it are given as worthy of imitation poems of no merit whatever and capable of perverting good taste; that its prologues are full of contradictions; that the discussions of the poets are inaccurate and in general too brief; that the indexes and judgments of the works in it, besides being almost entirely copied from elsewhere, give false ideas about poetry; that the style of Mr. Sedano has the vices of bad grammar, obscurity, improper choices of words . . . and finally that it needs orthographic corrections. I have said only a part of a great deal which occurs to me concerning that collection; and still I would not have said so much if Mr. Sedano had not provoked me to do so with the censure he has tried to make of my translation. . . . [23]

Iriarte also inserts some correspondence between Sedano and Vicente de los Ríos. The latter had sent Sedano some mild criticisms of the first volume of the *Parnassus*. Sedano replied in a quite patronizing fashion. Ríos sent these letters to Iriarte so that they could be published in this attack on a work and a man who had now begun to make vitriolic attacks on both Ríos and Iriarte.[24] Sedano's letters are intriguing in that they show Sedano's personality quite clearly. He writes less formally but even more heatedly, although he does manage to camouflage his wrath most of the time. Iriarte shows tremendous insight into the personality of Sedano, and near the end of the dialogue he states his belief in a surprisingly modern, analytical way:

The *Parnassian* gentleman wishes to be irreprehensible: he speaks of authors en masse; when he sees he is censured, he turns on the censor; and if on one hand he wants to back up the nonsense he has said, on the other hand he seeks to show that he already knew and showed, with no one else's help, the same defects that he had stated were perfections, thus falling into puerile and ridiculous contradictions. In short, he is one of those who, when they have made a blunder and some good soul points it out, respond with this or some other similar

pet phrase: "Well, that and what I said are all the same; we are in
agreement; yes, now there is no doubt, etc." But on entering a discourse again, since the reasons and the concept are borrowed, they
return to their old habits, they stumble, slip . . . and finally fall again
into the same error.[25]

Iriarte ends the long vindication of his translation by affirming,
as on other occasions, that he is glad he made his translation
whether he has done any service to his country or not. At least
he enjoyed his work and used his time more wisely than those
whose only occupation is to sit idly by and criticize what others
do. And he even anticipates the appearance of his *Fables* in a few
years when he concludes that these loafers are like the "useless
drones who disturb the industrious bees in their labor, and while
the latter strive to provide us with honey, they do nothing more
than cause confusion with their uncouth buzzing." [26]

The first and most visible result of Iriarte's dialogue was the
cessation of Sedano's labors on the *Parnassus.* No more volumes
ever appeared in this unfortunate venture. As far as Iriarte is
concerned, the dialogue shows how he reacted in his first important polemic—a reaction that is moderate and restrained. But
more important for us as readers of Iriarte today is that the dialogue and all that preceded it quite forcefully show us the
tremendous erudition of the writer. The facility with which he
handled the original Latin and converted it into Spanish cannot
be faulted. Such a statement must include our high regard for
the innovative mode of translating. The choice of Horace's work
and the way he follows the precepts therein in his translation are
significant for us as we seek to establish what Iriarte's goals and
literary credos were. At this initial stage in the production of his
important works we see that he is counselling prudence, moderation, and good taste. These characteristics carry over into the
dialogue where he responds directly and personally to his most
vehement attacker, for here we find the basic note is moderation.
Finally this dialogue proves to us the insight and literary acumen
of Iriarte. It is here that he shows at length all that he had learned
in the early training in the Classics provided by his uncle.

III   La música (Music)

The poem *La música (Music),* for the most part forgotten today, is one of the works to appear in the late 1770's and early

1780's that gave Iriarte great renown, although the popularity
of this particular poem was evident more in foreign countries
than in Spain itself. The work was finished in 1779 but did not
come out until 1780. It is long, containing an introduction, five
cantos, and copious notes, and is unique in Spanish literature.
Before noting one or two sketchy works that are hardly comparable to his own, Iriarte states why he undertook such an
unusual project: "[The motive] was principally the consideration
that among the arts and sciences which various geniuses both
Ancient and Modern have treated in didactic poems music should
have been slighted, this oversight seeming all the more unjust
since her sister, poetry, has merited having her doctrine explained
in verse by Horace, Vida, Boileau, and others." [27] The treatment
accorded music in this poem must at last rectify the oversight
because certainly little pertaining to that art has been overlooked
in this treatise. Not only is the coverage complete, it is organized
in such a fashion as to allow the reader to peruse the poem at
random and still discover the basic points of Iriarte's arguments.
There is first a very comprehensive introduction that tells in detail
what the cantos are about. Then each canto has a concise outline
of the subjects to be found in it. This attention to form and to the
easy comprehension of all material presented reminds the reader
that the poet is following the admonitions of his mentor, Horace.
After the publication of the translation of the *Poetics* therefore, the
assimilation of its tenets is total and is an essential part of Iriarte's
activity as a writer and critic. This almost unconscious imbibing
is another reason for considering Iriarte completely developed
as a writer by 1780 and for considering the works appearing in
the few years after 1777 as the fruition of youthful apprenticeship.
   The first canto is the most didactic and, as a result, difficult
to read. Basically it treats the essence of music—i.e., sound and
tempo. An apologetic tone is noted in the introduction where
Iriarte regrets the overwhelming dullness of this section: "This
first canto, as it is the basis for the four following and its purely
didactic context hardly permits the intrusion of any pleasant note,
demands more than anything the serious attention of the reader,
and must of necessity entertain him less than the others: just as
in good dramas the first act destined for the exposition of the
personality and situation of the characters necessarily requires
the most attention of the audience, instructing it before entertain-

ing it." [28] In the third division of this canto he launches into the truly didactic facet of his work and it is indeed difficult to maintain one's attention, but at the end of this same canto Iriarte, in a particularly lyrical outburst, laments the uselessness of all the precepts enumerated in this section of his poem if a composer lacks sensitivity and genius. Without these qualities a writer is incapable of understanding the songs of Nature and of transcribing them to paper or to an instrument and thus to the hearts of men.

The second canto is a continuation of the first in a way, in that the poet goes on with his discussion of the importance of expression on the part of the composer. In order to make his point more apparent he sets forth his ideas through the words of a shepherd, Salicio, who tells his beloved Crisea what the word *expression* means and what it consists of. The use of the pastoral setting for didactic purposes is intriguing. In all the work of Iriarte, and perhaps in all that of the eighteenth century, the idea of *utile dulci* is said nowhere so succinctly as here in this short section of his poem. With all the proper accoutrements of the typical pastoral setting, two young people sit down to teach and learn the importance of feeling and emotion in music. The attitude is summed up exactly in two lines preceding a very formal exposition: "How happy I shall be, if, as the art [of music] pleases,/ My teaching can also please you!" (*¡Felice yo, si, qual te agrada el arte,/ Mi enseñanza tambien puede agradarte!*).[29] At the end of the presentation of all the "doctrine," recalling the apologetic tone noted above in the introductory material for the first canto, Salicio begs Crisea to forgive him for tiring her with so much material and in particular for discussing funereal music. It was not this latter, he affirms, that made him the conqueror of her love but tender music that made her heart open to him. Thus again, we are given a sympathetic example of the poet's precepts. The two are portrayed, as the canto ends, infused with love and trust, completely lacking in artifice, disdain, or jealousy as they return to their village. In this segment Iriarte has magnificently combined the pastoral and bucolic (including the *beatus-ille* theme) with the didactic to present in a vivid example the value and importance of music and the emotions it can arouse.

The third canto is more diverse in makeup than the previous ones. The first section explains the types of music used in the

church, in the theater, and in both public and private performances. In other sections Iriarte discusses the music used in
church more fully, including such subjects as the quality of
voices that make up the choir, the instruments used in providing
the music, and the kinds of music which are performed in church.
In one section he discusses some famous Spanish composers of
earlier times. It is here that he praises Spanish music, for, more
than any other national expression, sacred music is the realm of
tremendous activity and wealth. Not only is the production of
sacred music one of Spain's great contributions to herself, it is
perhaps the greatest gift of Spain to Western civilization. Certainly this is one of the first times such an assertion is made,
preceding by many years more modern recognition of this great
heritage from Spain. In the last section Iriarte exhorts youth to
study music so as to continue the fame that Spain already enjoys
in this art. His tone becomes almost political when he holds
Charles III up to his readers as an example. He asserts that the
King will generously protect those who take up a career in music,
and he looks into the future when he expects to see music ennobled and placed on a level with the sciences and fine arts already enjoying the patronage of the monarch.

The fourth canto is devoted mainly to music in the theater, i.e.,
opera or melodrama. After speaking of its origins, Iriarte discusses how opera has undergone a renovation in his own century,
going into some detail about Metastasio and how much he has
done for the ennobling of this particular art. From here he goes
into a poetic fantasy where the Italian composer Niccolò Jommèlli leads him through the Elysian Fields. This episode naturally recalls the epic device of the descent into the underworld.
Here the wanderer is vouchsafed visions of composers from the
past. Jommèlli, only recently deceased, explains the state of music
in his own day. The passage is a novel usage of an ancient literary
device, and Iriarte uses it to best advantage by letting Jommèlli
proceed with his account saying only that he regrets not being
able to relate what he heard in as beautiful a style as Jommèlli's
(a facetious statement since Iriarte has written both Jommèlli's
and his own words). He returns ultimately to the real world to
give his own comments on the state of the *zarzuela* (operetta) in
Spain, lamenting the fact that Jommèlli was not Spanish so as to
have known and praised this worthy contribution of Spanish

music. The notes in the appendix at the end of the poem include a precise, detailed biography of Jommèlli. The value of Iriarte's method, the *utile dulci,* is thus seen first in the poetic descent to an underworld which is then accompanied by a learned explanation of who the writer's guide was.

The fifth canto concerns music as entertainment in small gatherings or in solitude. The poet praises academies of music, discusses the various forms this type of music may take, lauds the Germans and principally among them Joseph Haydn, and ends with a gathering of the Arts presided over by Good Taste. The latter proposes the establishment of an Academy of Music. The proposal is met with the approval of all attending and each one (Painting, Sculpture, Architecture, Engraving, Poetry, and Eloquence) offers to contribute to the advancement and honor of her sister, Music. In the appendix Iriarte inserts a curious note wherein he defends his personifying the arts: "When in the Royal Academy of San Fernando the public and solemn distribution of prizes is celebrated it is the custom to read poems and orations in praise of the noble Arts, it is thus not a poetic fiction to introduce Poetry and Oratory here as witnesses of that act." [30]

At the end of his notes for this canto he includes a long treatise on the suitability of the Spanish language for the composition of songs. This is a fitting conclusion to the work because it unites Iriarte's knowledge of the history of music, his understanding of musical terms and expressions, and his feeling for the essence of music and what it must portray to an audience if it is to be truly effective. But to state succinctly what the real intention of his entire poem is we return to a statement in the introduction:

I therefore trust that most readers will acquire a decent knowledge of certain fine points which . . . are denied those less well versed in music or that at least they will come to possess a more noble idea of it than that which those badly organized persons have who disdaining the beauties of the fine arts try to take their revenge on Nature who created them incapable of feeling such beauties. If I obtain this end that I have particularly proposed for myself, I shall hold my task well carried out, feeling myself useful in something even at the cost of erring in a great deal.[31]

In this chapter we have been concerned with three works by Iriarte that indicate the attainment of his maturation as a writer.

That the first is a translation of Horace's *Poetics* is important because it shows the culmination of all his early training in the Classics and is a natural result of the discipline experienced in his first, most formative years. The translation is significant too because it indicates who will be his true mentor and artistic guide throughout the rest of his life. The points that we chose to comment on from the *Poetics* are significant because they prove so concisely what the basic motivations were in Iriarte's concept of writing. The translation is also important because it ultimately involved Iriarte in the series of polemics that were to plague him for the rest of his life. His well-developed essay is a gem in the history of literary polemics. It succeeds in destroying the adversary, but even more positively it adds new facts about certain aspects of Spanish literature hitherto not publicized. Its style demonstrates the teachings of Horace, those of moderation and restraint. At this point in his career Iriarte has succeeded in assimilating his master's precepts to the extent they are now his own. He is able to build upon them by producing a work of true merit. This achievement is amply proved by the publication of a unique poem that seeks to teach and entertain, the two basic tenets of Classical literature so much desired by all Neoclassic artists. Again, that Iriarte is able to achieve these ends while producing a work that is totally new in concept and scope is all the more commendable. By this time (1780) he is not just a mere translator of plays (an occupation that gained him some notice in the early 1770's) or even a deft translator of Horace. He has definitively entered the world of fertile literary composition on his own terms. His manner of writing is established, although his style and choice of subject are still apparently more popular outside than inside his own country. His mordant wit is already gaining him enemies who will continue to lacerate him in turn. He has thus reached a tone and direction in his life that will never really desert him. He is ready to produce his best-known work, the *Fábulas literarias (Literary Fables),* basing himself on his talents and resources now fully developed and capable of carrying him on to greater heights.

CHAPTER 3

The *Fábulas literarias*

I *Form of the* Literary Fables

IN his study of Molière and Florian and their indebtedness to certain Spanish writers, François Vézinet betrays a not unexpected condescending French attitude toward these same writers. He has a great deal to say about the debt of Florian to Iriarte when writing his own *Fables,* but he still manages to make Iriarte sound almost inferior to the French writer. This infuriating tendency of the critic is somewhat modified in one place where he discovers the real contribution of Iriarte to Spanish letters of the eighteenth century: "The superiority of Iriarte?" he writes, "It rests above all in his invention. He imagines and then invents his subjects." [1] As we shall find in the last chapter of the present study of Iriarte, critics have tended to go to extremes in their criticism of the fabulist—either praising him extravagantly or failing to find much of value in his work. Vézinet hits upon a happy compromise here, perhaps unintentionally, of penetrating to the core of Iriarte's importance and then succinctly stating it. His assertion is valid because it relates the most significant quality of the *Literary Fables.* Iriarte's "inventiveness" is most visible in the selection of the genre of the fable to expound his views. The fable is of itself naturally didactic and yet it can be among the most entertaining of all types of literature. In the mere choice of vehicle we see that Iriarte is following his guide, Horace, whose work he had translated only some five years earlier.

In the first chapter the background and history of the *Fables* were given at some length. The intention now is to see more closely what the *Fables* are about. The editor's short preface to the first edition (included in the 1787 edition of the complete works which is used here) states why this work was published in 1782. The seemingly simple declaration of the editor was soon to create a storm of controversy, however:

Because some imperfect and adulterated copies of these fables were beginning to wander about in the hands of the curious, it seemed to me that I would do the literary public a service by asking their author for them, taking advantage of the friendship which I have with him, and by bringing them to light with his approval. I do not wish to prejudice the readers' judgment about their merit; but only to advise those least versed in our literature that this is the first collection of entirely original fables that has been published in Spanish. [It was this sentence that so infuriated Samaniego and began the polemic mentioned in our Chapter 1.] And thus as it has for Spain this particular recommendation, it has even another for foreign nations: that is, the novelty of all its themes being related to literature. The inventors of fables that are solely moral of course have found characteristics in animals that can be easily applied to human defects as regards customs, because animals have their passions as well; but as the latter do not read or write, it was much more difficult to find in them particulars that could have some relation with literary vices or with the precepts that should serve as a norm for writers.[2]

It is true obviously that Iriarte is not the originator of the fable, but he is the first and only one in Western European literature to leave an extensive *original* collection of them. This is the point Vézinet was making. It is what the editor is trying to say, a bit ineptly, as well. The editor's somewhat naïve generosity may have been well founded but it caused much unwanted hardship for Iriarte later. Had he better clarified what he meant by "first collection of entirely original fables," the unhappy rift between Samaniego and Iriarte would have been avoided, as well as the acerbic controversy with Forner perhaps.

A part of such an introduction that might be expected and is indeed notably lacking is a statement concerning the goals of the author in writing his work. The editor does note, however, one very useful attribute of this collection and that is the variety of poetic meters to be encountered in the fables, and he adds that there is even an index of these meters at the end. The editor, again rather innocuously, states that this index will be of help to young poets. There are some forty types of meter. For the most part the verses range from four to as many as fourteen syllables, the most popular being the hendecasyllable, the octosyllable, the heptasyllable, and the hexasyllable. We soon discover moreover that while employing all these forms Iriarte did not so much intend a renovation of the forms of Spanish poetry as a simple display of its variety and richness. And even though his purpose in varying his meters was to show the versatility of Spanish, it is interesting to see that he did have preferences and an evident dexterity in manipulating some poetic forms over others. For example, the shorter verse forms are fewer in number, but are nevetherless more effective. The poet also returns to old Spanish forms quite regularly—the *silva*, the *romance*, and the *redondilla* are much in evidence. The assonant verse form is popular in the fables too. Iriarte has provided in his collection not only a proper homage to the multitude of Spanish verse forms; he has created a veritable monument to his own skill in using these forms.

II *Allusions to Contemporaries*

One reason for the immediate success of the *Fables* was that they were believed to contain references to contemporary figures. Many people rushed to obtain a copy of the work simply to see whether they could ascertain who might be the subject of a particular fable. It was extremely difficult then, and more so now, to know precisely whether Iriarte was criticizing certain enemies and the follies they committed. Forner asserted that Iriarte had written at the end of each fable the name of the person being ridiculed.[3] Forner's statement sounds quite typical of his usual fulminations against Iriarte, however. It must be admitted that his words and those of others sound more like jealous mouthings than anything else. Iriarte's critics were extremely notable because of their loudness which often covered up a lack of self-assuredness —and of truth. Since the "subjects" of these fables have never been acceptably determined by the critics, it seems that readers will have to be content with believing what they want regarding the allusions—or else with dismissing the entire question as of little importance when confronted with the true literary value of the fables themselves. Yet because the critics' assertions are significant from an historical, critical, and biographical point of view, we must consider some of their ideas here.

In his incisive essay which appeared in 1867 Francisco Fernández González, whether intentionally or not, sums up indirectly some of the allusions most generally accepted by the mid-nineteenth century: ". . . he [Iriarte] may speak by means of transparent allusions of Huerta, whom he converts into a duck, or of Samaniego metamorphosed at will into a rat, a ferret, and a

seasoner of eggs; or he may seem to give to the works of Ramón
de la Cruz the importance given to the comings and goings of the
squirrel; or he may direct to his own friend Vicente de los Ríos
the little poems about the rooster, the pig, and the lamb, as a
corrective for his singular opinions. . . ." [4] There were more allusions believed by the general public, but these few serve as a
résumé of how the early readers interpreted what they saw.

References can be seen in the *Fables* too that reflect a great
deal of the bitterness felt by Iriarte after he had begun to
publish his works definitively. There is no specific mention of a
name, but the subject of two fables (XXII and XXIII) in particular sounds a great deal like Sedano, the editor of the ill-fated
Spanish Parnassus:

> There is a set of dastard knaves,
> Vile critics, that will wait to make attack
> On authors till their victims are—alack!—
> All safe and quiet in their graves;
> For living men, they know, might answer back.

And even though, again it must be repeated, Iriarte makes no
specific mention of anyone, he did evidently have someone in
mind:

> Denounced though I may be,
> By coward critics, that I here expose—
> Because I dare their meanness to disclose;
> Their portrait they shall see
> In yet another fable ere I close.[5]

The business here sounds very similar to all the troubles he
had suffered at the hands of Sedano and the first quotation could
very well be considered a reference to the malicious attack by
Sedano on Vicente de los Ríos after his death. If this is all meant
to be an attack on Sedano, we can see quite succinctly then
Iriarte's anger and frustration because of this man. There is
perhaps a further castigation of Sedano in number XL, but its
moral could easily apply to various people. In this fable two
travelers have spent the night in two different inns—both exactly
opposite to what they appear on the outside. Iriarte concludes:

A portal tall and sightly,
Within inclement garrets,
With tiled roof covered slightly.
Its inmate comfortless,
Did a weary sojourn make;
And bewailed unto his comrade,
Next day, his sad mistake.
His friend thus answer gives:
"In like manner many a book
Its reader's hopes deceives." [6]

Conceivably Iriarte could be referring to the *Spanish Parnassus,* that colossal structure constructed by Sedano, but it is almost belaboring the point to declare for certain it is Sedano to whom Iriarte makes reference. This fable does confront us with the basic problem of the so-called allusions in these poems. Sedano could be the target of the moral, but a great many other writers might be also. To insist on one particular writer, as so many of the early readers and critics did, is to charge Iriarte with licentiousness, and such a charge cannot reasonably be made. The efforts of so many early critics to discredit Iriarte by saying his work was merely a malicious vehicle for attacking his contemporaries in many cases, therefore, had very doubtful foundations or bases in fact.

Continuing in this same vein of thought, we must question the assertion that number XLVI ("The Cocks") is a reference to someone in particular. Its subject is undeniably one that caused Iriarte much concern, however:

A Cock, that was well known
As a champion brave and stout,
And a Chicken but half grown
Squabbled something about,
But what, to me's unknown,
And, after furious din,
At last got up a very pretty battle;
In which the chick such fight did show,
And the old one around so sharply rattle,
That, with a loud, exultant crow,
He claimed the honors of the field to win.
Then the seraglio's vanquished lord,
His rival out of hearing of his tongue,

Said, "Ah! in time he'll make a pretty bird,
But, now, poor fellow, he is very young."
No more he dared himself to match
With the young hero; but again
With an old Cock he had a scratch,
Of many fights, a veteran,
Who hardly left him plume or crest.
Whereon he muttered to the rest,
"The fine old fellow!—surely it would be
Unfair to thrash so old a chap as he."

Let him that will in strife engage
On any question literary,
Pay less attention to the age
Than talents of his adversary.[7]

Rather than declaring that Sedano was the subject of this poem, the critics would have done much more good pointing out the strong emotion and frustration inherent in the words of Iriarte. To whomever the fable is directed, if at all to any one specific person, it is most important for showing us the vulnerability felt by the poet when exposed to older, more established writers, albeit less talented now because of their senility. This human, very personal characteristic is immediately evident in addition to the literary moral the fable preaches. It is these personal and moral attributes of the poem that should interest the reader and not the possible object of its teachings.

There were other writers whose views, or whose works expounding these views, were supposedly anathema to Iriarte. Two of these will suffice—Ramón de la Cruz for his ideas on the theater and Juan Meléndez Valdés for his poetic language. It is true that there was personal antagonism on the part of Iriarte toward these authors, but it was directed for the most part against their modes of expression, so different from his own. Fable XXVIII, although it never mentions Ramón de la Cruz, contains Iriarte's basic criticism of the contemporary traditionalist drama and dramatists of whom the leading exponent was Cruz. The words of this particular fable could directly assail that popular playwright if one should so choose to consider the poem:

"On good and bad an equal value sets
The stupid mob. From me the worst it gets,

And never fails to praise." With vile pretence,
The scurrilous author thus his trash excused.
A poet shrewd, hearing the lame defence,
Indignant, thus exposed the argument abused.
A Donkey's master said unto his beast,
While doling out to him his lock of straw,
"Here, take it—since such diet suits your taste,
And much good may it do your vulgar maw!"
Often the slighting speech the man repeated.
The Ass—his quiet mood by insult heated—
Replies: "Just what you choose to give, I take,
Master unjust! But not because I choose it.
Think you I nothing like but straw? Then make
The experiment. Bring corn, and see if I refuse it."

Ye caterers for the public, hence take heed
How your defaults by false excuse you cover!
Fed upon straw—straw it may eat, indeed:
Try it with generous fare—'twill scorn the other.[8]

Herein lies the basic creed of Iriarte concerning the contemporary drama—that the public should be given decent presentations on the stage empty of all the extravagance and exaggeration that had reigned in Spanish plays for nearly two hundred years. The abuse he cites here is one he and all the Neoclassic dramatists had been fighting for some time. When the reader considers this point, the question of who the person alluded to is becomes less relevant.

A similar reaction is felt when one examines the fables that supposedly were directed against Meléndez Valdés. It will be remembered from Chapter 1 that Iriarte had become rather irritated with Meléndez, admittedly somewhat unreasonably, over the latter's success with his poem that won the Academy's award for 1779. Fable XXXIX was thought to be directed against the at times archaic, and as a result stilted and false, language employed by Meléndez and others of his circle. It is entitled "The Portrait" and involves a young painter who felt that to be worthy a portrait must contain all the characteristics of the painting of a Vclázquez. He therefore painted his subject in the dress and appearance of a man of the early seventeenth century. The patron, naturally taken aback, paid his artist with old, worthless coins, saying: "as you've painted me, so I have paid you." The literary abuse Iriarte is condemning is explained in the introduction and in the moral at the end:

A spreading contagion, defacing our tongue
With phrases outlandish, our critics bemoan.
But some fools have their notions of purity hung
Upon obsolete terms superseding our own.
Living words they despise as a vulgar intrusion,
And forgotten ones rake from oblivion's gloom.
For a word of advice on such stupid conclusion,
In phrase like their own, we here must find room;
In two dialects, jostling in motley confusion. . . .
Hold, now. If we laugh at the farcical notion
Of this modern Painter, and deem it so droll,
Why may we not laugh at the Author's devotion,
His ideas who drapes in antiquity's stole;
Who shocks us with phrases all moldy with age;
Thinks oddity graceful; and purity's self
Considers his style, when he darkens his page
With expressions forgotten and laid on the shelf;
And believes that no term by pure taste is forbid,
If it only were good in the time of the Cid? [9]

Cotarelo believes, in addition, that one of the fables published after Iriarte's death alludes to Meléndez, especially as its theme is the same as the one just cited. Of the fables published posthumously two were written in verse and one in prose. The one referred to here would be number LXVIII and would be the first of the two. Its prose explanation declares: "Those who mix archaic words with those of good [modern] use, to credit themselves with writing their language well, write it badly and make themselves ridiculous." [10] Surely, however, the ideas concerning style of writing, the basis of a polemic throughout the entire eighteenth century, are more important than who were the persons referred to in the fables.

While on the subject of allusions, we should consider briefly the third of these posthumously published fables. It is in prose and almost certainly refers to Iriarte himself:

There was a Canary who, having taken pains to improve his song, succeeded in pleasing certain people and he began to receive applause. . . . What the Canary won . . . [however] . . . excited the envy of some birds. Among these were some who also sang, well or badly, and because of this they persecuted him. Others could not sing at all and for this reason they hated him. Finally, a Crow who could not shine by himself, tried to become famous by beginning to scream publicly among the birds against the Canary. . . . The Canary, bored, no longer wanted to sing; until the Eagle, queen of the birds, ordered him to sing to see whether, indeed, he brayed [like a donkey—the calumny spread by the Crow] or not. . . . The Canary opened his beak and sang to the pleasure of most of the listeners. Then the Eagle, indignant at the slander spread by the Crow, called upon the god Jupiter to punish him. The god agreed and told the Eagle to order the Crow to sing. But when the latter tried to, he began by royal permission to bray horrendously. All the animals laughed and said: "With good reason he who tried to make an ass of the Canary has become one himself." [11]

The suffering caused by the attacks on his personality, his ability, and his work is all too evident here. The crow is probably Forner. Throughout the fables published posthumously there is a tendency to refer to the canary frequently. In this case one is forced to agree that there do seem to be specific allusions.

The question of the allusions of the *Literary Fables* is indeed intriguing as can be seen from the few examples provided. And yet the value of the poems does not lie in their providing some sort of guessing game. To dwell on the question of allusions is to continue to meander through a maze trod by critics for nearly two hundred years. Without being able to determine definitely who the subjects were—if any reference to a living person was actually intended in all the cases cited by innumerable critics—it is unwise to let these identifications become the main subject of consideration. And yet, after all the hesitation and doubt concerning this aspect, one is obliged to admit that the question of allusions can be made pertinent in one major way. As noted earlier, it is this aspect of the work that caused it to gain much of its initial popularity and pushed Iriarte's name even higher in literary circles. The possibility of slander or mere gossip and of the public airing of a person's insecurities (such qualities can be seen in some of the poems quoted above, particularly number XLVI) is always enough to entice a willing and waiting audience. Many believed the proposed identifications by Forner and others who harbored grudges against the poet.

It is no wonder then that the rash of diatribes and polemics occurred. This outpouring of invective is the most visible and direct result of the supposed allusions in the *Fables*. The case of the allusions ironically can be considered fertile in that it did cause two works to be produced, *The Erudite Ass* of Forner and *For Just Such Cases Do They Have Trained Teachers* written in response by Iriarte. *For Just Such Cases* is valuable today because it serves as a kind of prose commentary on the *Fables*, explaining what criticisms were meant in certain instances. In an indirect way some good does come from this polemic, therefore, but as usual it has to come in an almost perverse way. There are other polemics, such as the one with Samaniego, although it is caused for other reasons. They all end up putting Iriarte on the defensive, or at least in a position where he must reply to his accusers. In his reply he elaborates as to what the purposes of the *Fables* were —a question that we must consider now in some detail.

III   *Purpose of the* Literary Fables

It was stated earlier that there is no real introduction to the *Literary Fables*. The first fable does present some of the author's basic points in embryo form; he even prefaces it with the word *Prologue*. The Elephant is portrayed as the wisest of the beasts in this poem. It is he who realizes the state of disrepair that language is in at the moment:

> In careful phrase, well learned by heart,
> Long years ago, in far-off land,
> When every brute beast had a way,
> What he thought and felt, to say
> In language all could understand—
> The sagacious Elephant observed
> Among these creatures many a failing,
> And gross abuses, too, prevailing,
> Which strenuous reform deserved.
> He called them all, from far and near,
> His strictures on their ways to hear.
> With reverence the most profound
> His long proboscis swept the ground;
> In careful phrase, well learned by heart,
> He then discharged the censor's part—
> A thousand silly foibles noted,

A thousand vicious actions quoted;
Envy, working sore vexation,
Ostentatious insolence,
Idleness, procrastination,
The arrogance of ignorance.

His sound and noble counsel stirs
The hearts of many listeners,
Accepting, with due reverence,
The dictates of his generous sense.
The guileless Lamb and thrifty Ant,
The Bee, frugal and provident,
The trusty Setter, and the Dove,
Ever faithful to her love,
The obedient Horse, the Linnet shy,
And the simple Butterfly.
But, of the audience, a part not small
Declared that their offended pride
Such language plain could not abide;
Not they—no, not at all.
The Tiger and rapacious Wolf,
Opening their lank jaws' bloody gulf,
Against the adviser rave;
His vile abuse, among the crowd,
The venomous Serpent hissed aloud;
While, all around, the whispering tone
Of Wasp and Hornet, Fly and Drone,
A murmuring echo gave.
The mischievous Balm-cricket leapt
From the tumultuous throng;
The Locust spread his clanging wing,
His greedy conscience felt the sting;
The wriggling Caterpillar crept
His sneaking way along;
The Weasel arched his spiteful back;
The Fox kept silence shrewd;
The Monkey, sauciest of the pack,
Mocked, with grimaces rude.

The stately Elephant looked down
Upon the vexed turmoil:
"To each and all and yet to none,"
Spake his calm voice above the broil,
"These censures I apply;

Let him who winces put them on;
Who not, hear quietly."

Whoever may my fables read,
This truth important let him heed:
That to all nations—not to any one—
And to all times, they speak.
The world has shown alike
The faults at which they strike
In each revolving week.
Then—since the warning finger
Points at no destined head—
Who feels the censure linger
Must sup on his own bread.[12]

Among all the vitriol that *For Just Such Cases* contains, the really clarifying statements made by Iriarte readily stand out. It is thus here that we find an elaboration of Iriarte's purpose which is rather implied than stated in the fables themselves as best evidenced in the poem just quoted. The polemical work *For Just Such Cases* is in the form of a letter to Iriarte written by Eleuterio Geta, a supposedly close friend who of course is Iriarte himself. Don Eleuterio proceeds quite logically to urge Iriarte to react to Forner's malicious fable *The Erudite Ass*. After giving many examples of uncalled-for provocation on the part of Forner, Don Eleuterio begins to note at various intervals what Iriarte's purposes in writing were. They are actually simple amplifications of the statements in the fable about the elephant. At one point Don Eleuterio quotes from Forner himself to show rather ingeniously what the *Fables* really are:

"And what is the teaching they announce to us? Perhaps the intimate delicacies of the Arts; the ways for finding the truth among so many doubts; the certain resolution of the opinions that tire human understanding so much? Not at all, not at all. These bagatelles are good only for a Doctor Gothic, or for an insipid and silly Scholastic. They teach. . . . They teach what they can: general, common things that anyone knows without study and therefore without the necessity for tiring oneself in reading bad verses. . . . They teach, for example: *That it is better to do one thing well than many badly; That he who works without the rules of art succeeds only by chance, if he succeeds at all. . . . That a nicely bound book can be poorly written; That a*

house can have a good façade and a horrible interior [italics of
Iriarte]. Good Lord! What new and useful discoveries for the good
of man!" [Don Eleuterio, i.e., Iriarte, goes on in his brilliant way to
dismiss the sarcasm of the comments and to put them to his own use]
It seems . . . that the delicate taste of Mr. Pablo Segarra [Forner] is
not satisfied with those clear and simple truths that we read in all the
philosophers, in the books of Christian ethics, and significantly in the
fabulists. The moral truths of Aesop are all very natural and quite
trivial. . . .[13]

Basically the passage just quoted shows what the simple purpose of Iriarte's work is—to give some kind of logic and reason
to the Spanish language that Iriarte feels is still too full of the
empty exuberance and exaggeration left from the excesses of the
Gongoristic-Conceptistic schools of the previous century. One
could go further perhaps and say that Iriarte also wishes to
provide certain logical, reasonable restraints on the Spanish
character in general, for the themes of some of the fables are more
than literary. In any case, the purpose is so simple that it can
astonish the reader if he stops to think about it because common
sense should have told him long ago that no such rules should be
necessary. Iriarte portrays Forner as the most stupid of contemporary offenders because he mouths the protestations of those
who do not see the unfortunate state of affairs. By using Forner's
own words that were originally to have ridiculed Iriarte, the
latter adroitly turns the tables on his critic. Earlier Don Eleuterio
had labelled Forner as one of the unenlightened, using the term
Gothic that becomes so popular with the Romantics. He relegates
Forner to that age of darkness and ignorance which was particularly abhorrent to the enlightened eighteenth-century gentleman—the Middle Ages or Gothic period. Here he uses the word
Gothicism to refer to what that period evoked in the eighteenth-
century mind. His contemporaries who are guilty of reflecting the
ignorance and dullness of that time are also referred to pejora-
tively:

The new fabulist [Forner] is annoyed that you [Iriarte] in your
Fable LXV have declared yourself against *Gothicism*, or Gothic taste.
What is thus called *Gothicism* in literature and the fine arts is well
known. Every educated man knows and abhors that mortal enemy of
the arts [who is always] so very bitter and dreadful that when he

[the enemy] gains entrance into the republic of the sciences, he banishes good taste, and with it reason, sometimes for centuries. Then the Segarras, taking absolute control, adulterate it, overturn it, and contaminate it. Then the undigestible farrago of all that species occupies the seat of the Humanities. Disorder is introduced; the laws, with the abolition of the most fundamental, wise, and beneficial, are broken and despised; and only foolish and monstrous Caprice reigns, sustained by idleness and ignorance. How thankful we should be to you for having made war on the said *Gothicism* with that fable! And it does not matter that . . . Segarra pretends that you despise the study of the sciences and that you direct your apologues against them when no one will be able to read them with good intentions who does not see that in them, quite on the contrary, one is exhorted to study the sciences themselves . . . and only the vices that are introduced into them are reprehended. You should have the satisfaction of knowing that your fables are having the desired effect of wounding the Ignorant, the Farraguists, the Scholastic Disputants, combatting their false and uncouth principles.[14]

Iriarte manifests so well the "enlightened" attitude of his century in the above comment. His detestation of the Dark Ages or Middle Ages (both terms usually being equally pejorative in their application) marks him clearly among those writers and thinkers possessing the most "modern" attitude of his day. To many of Iriarte's contemporaries that earlier period was abhorrent because of its refusal to admit the possibilities of Man and its resultant failure to advance Man's state. That Iriarte names Forner as the worst of the offenders who commit the same errors as those of that Dark Age indicates the idea held by Iriarte about all those reactionary Traditionalists who refused to admit anything new in the Spanish language or customs. It is against the Forners that all the enlightened Spaniards have been fighting for a century, Iriarte is saying. One almost senses a near panic and hopelessness on his part, as if he and all his predecessors have been fighting in vain to overcome the Gothic darkness that will not leave the Spanish atmosphere, whether it be in its language or some other manifestation. But with characteristic verve he regains control of himself and waxes optimistic at the end of the quotation. In miniature we find Iriarte well portrayed here: the fiery, determined, and idealistic reformer who nearly despairs at the severe attacks by his enemies but who rallies as always and returns to the fray.

This is a multifaceted essay; it is a diatribe, but it is also an explanation of the writer's beliefs—and of his own mission.

Elaborating on his purposes in writing, Iriarte returns specifically to his cardinal point that a writer, or any artist, must follow certain rules. This idea, a part of both his early conscious and subconscious development, first became strikingly evident through his translation of the *Poetics,* as we noted in the previous chapter. As was indicated then, all the basic tenets of Horace became Iriarte's since he had been exposed to them all his life. That he should express these same ideas in his most personally creative work is not at all unusual. The *Fables* then are a sort of homage to his master. Here in this critical essay he is essentially telling us that the rules of Nature must apply to all forms of writing, and, carrying his exhortation further, to all aspects of human existence. The statements tell us that simplicity, measure, and inherent common sense are those qualities that must always be sought after. If not, he again points out, the result is confusion and chaos and final defeat. The following quotation, written in specific response to a statement by Forner that no rules are necessary for writing fables except that of whim or caprice, is particularly appropriate: "[If the fable does not follow constant rules based on the observation of Nature and on the great poets who knew how to imitate Her with propriety,] Then what will it be? A dream of one in delirium, a monster, a confused fabrication; in sum, a *Caprice,* a fable like that of the *Erudite Ass* which does not observe the rules of quantity or those of quality that every well-made fable must observe. Before having pronounced such an absolute maxim, the author should have read and reread the masters of the poetic art and he would have seen then whether or not there are rules for writing fables." Iriarte (in the guise of Don Eleuterio) goes on to castigate Forner for the poor construction and ridiculous verbiage in his fable and in all his writing, and in that of all those whom Forner represents:

This is what happens to those who write without rules, who scorn art. I can only think of the ropewalker who intending to be a good equilibrist dropped his balancing pole and had already fallen to the ground when he heard that salutary maxim: "Will you flee art and method? Well, my son,/This will not be your last bump." [Fable LX]. If one of those who write without rules does succeed in saying something that is not an absurdity, he will have the same fortune as that Ass (not the *Erudite* one but the *Flutist* [Fable VIII]) who . . . caused the flute to play by chance with an accidental snort. Besides all this, I ask: how will he who wants to prove your fables bad do so without judging them according to the established principles of poetry? Will it be enough that what he says is bad is bad, or what is good will be so because some friend of yours says it is? Caprice will decide all that, and we shall defend the literary laws with sticks as the law of Mohammed is defended.[15]

At the end of this long treatise, Iriarte reviews his feelings. He at first appears to submit to the tremendous opposition he has aroused, but, as noted earlier, he refuses to do so because deep inside he knows he is right. His efforts and his expected accomplishments will live on, he feels, and with determination goading him on he will not listen to his detractors or be moved by their libelous attacks. Eleuterio speaks:

Let us be clear, my friend [Iriarte]: Do you want to live in an Augustan peace and placate your detractors? It is wholly within your power. Give them the pleasure of becoming bored; become unconcerned yourself; renounce the unfortunate poetic "sect"; and if some time you should feel the temptation to write, let it be only to become a Farraguist; compose some lowly book that will give no cause for one to think . . . and then I bet you will see your most turbulent, sullen, and rude antagonists become happy, courteous, and considerate. There is no other means of reforming your life so that they will pardon you for the unexpected temerity to have dared to write something new. But finally do be consoled by knowing that if among your readers there are tigers or wolves who become irritated, poisonous snakes who vomit forth insults, drones or gadflies who buzz with harsh voices, and all the other ugly creatures you portray in the first of your fables, there are also innocent lambs, loyal setters, industrious bees, and other little animals of good disposition as you yourself have duly noted.[16]

By now it is clear that the purposes of the *Fables* all point to one thing—a restoration of order and symmetry in language essentially, but Iriarte would not deny that these qualities are needed in all the arts and in life in general. This purpose then is what should concern the reader, Iriarte would have us believe, and not whether the *Fables* are directed against certain people. As he points out on several occasions: if the reader finds himself guilty of any of Iriarte's criticisms, then let him accept his guilt but know that he is not necessarily the target of the author's shafts.

IV *Themes of the* Fables

The themes of the fables naturally mirror their basic purpose. In general they all reflect it in some way even though a few admittedy do not deal directly with literary matters. It is possible, however, to separate the main directions of the moral truths so as to understand better what Iriarte was about and how he set forth his ideas. After studying the poems with some detail one finds that there are four general categories. There are some poems that do not fit together too well and nearly defy all attempts to classify them. The resulting difficulty, since it occurs rarely, however, need not deter our studying them in an organized way. The four categories are roughly as follows: (1) style, (2) the Traditionalists versus the Moderns, (3) the mentality of the mass man, and (4) the meaning of criticism. It will immediately be seen that there can be much overlapping of ideas among these classifications.

We may begin the study of Iriarte's idea of style with a fable noted before, number LX, concerning the ropedancer. In his index to the *Fables* at the end Iriarte notes: "In nothing can he advance who does not subject himself to rules." Basic to his beliefs about literary style there is that idea inherent in him from all his years of study of the Classics, i.e., the submission to limits and guidelines. In this same grouping number LI, entitled "The Lace-Makers," naturally follows in thought the one just noted. The poet here proclaims that the subject matter alone of a work is not enough; the method of treating it must be equally good:

> "For skill is known to all
> To be of greater worth than raw material."

> Let those, at style who sneer,
> And, to regard the matter only, condescend,
> Note that—as here
> A simple thread doth precious gold transcend—
> So elegance and finish give
> That form to thought, by which great works shall live.[17]

The theme is continued a few pages further on in number LIV:

> Nor does Genius aught avail
> Without the aid of Art.
> Long as they work apart,
> They both are sure to fail.[18]

Fable XXIX, "The Turnspit and the Mule of the Well," deals with a dog who turned a spit. Discontented, he escapes and encounters a mule who turns a wheel drawing water from a well. Thinking he will be more greatly rewarded for the greater task, he is sadly disillusioned by the mule:

> "To the spit and kitchen fire
> I advise you to go back.
> A turnspit strength would lack
> For the task to which you aspire."
>
> Now hear the Mule sagacious!
> Wisely, sure, he counsels thus;
> And one Horatius Flaccus
> This same matter does discuss.
> How idly doth an author yearn
> To undertake, where he must fail!
> The little Dog cannot avail
> The huge well-wheel to turn.[19]

The old, quite sane admonition to know one's limits surely holds here. Iriarte is indeed giving plain, simple truths.

Number XX, "The Bee and the Cuckoo," exhorts the writer to exhibit variety in his work. It is well to be useful like the bee, but in a work designed to please the senses invention is essential. Iriarte in number X declares that the work a writer produces must be his own. He uses the herb thyme as his model because, though small, she lives by her own abilities and is fertile and pleasing as opposed to the wallflower who grows only by the support of another. No one can hope to be considered a real author if nothing more is done than to insert an insipid prologue or notes into another's book. This admonition is extremely intriguing and even unexpected since it hits at the basis of some of those most productive labors of the eighteenth century. Emphasizing his love for simplicity and clarity in writing, Iriarte composes the

fable, "The Showman's Monkey and His Master" (VI), in which
the Monkey pretends to be as learned as his master. He does
quite well until he uses the magic lantern which he forgets to
light; no one sees anything although he discourses at great
length: "Pardon my hint, ye deep and subtile [sic] writers,/ Who
boast to be beyond our comprehensions;/ Your brains are dark
as the unlighted lanthorn." [20]

Turning to a question of style that was seen earlier in the
fable supposedly alluding to Meléndez Valdés, we find in LV,
"The Judge and the Robber," that habit or custom must not be
allowed to authorize what reason condemns. In this fable the
robber says that he should not be punished because all his life
he has practiced his "art" and ought not to be upbraided now.
Iriarte then says:

> Do we the bandit's wretched plea allow?
> Yet writers give no worthier excuse,
> Who justify, by argument of use,
> Errors of speech or of expression low—
> Urging the long-lived blunders of the past
> Against the verdict by sound critics cast.[21]

Fable V, "The Two Parrots and the Magpie," illustrates another
viewpoint while going essentially to the root of the same problem.
It is a question noted with and after Feijoo, i.e., the matter
of the "Frenchifying" of the Spanish language. In the fable one
parrot is French and another, Spanish. The latter imitates the
former in all respects until one day he finally emits some mongrel
French. A Magpie laughs at him, which elicits a haughty,
pompous reply: " 'You are nothing but a Purist,/ Of taste foolishly
exclusive.'/ 'Thanks for the compliment,' quoth Magpie, curtly." [22]
The concept of *purist* is not bad, therefore, when it stands in
sharp contrast to ignorance. Again the subtlety of Iriarte is immediately noticeable. The way in which he manages to maintain
a straight line between the pro- and anti-Gaulists is striking.
What he has to say on this same subject in *For Just Such Cases*
where he is more specific in his war on both camps enhances his
position all the more as a critic: "Add to this that just as those
antipurists against whom you so correctly direct the fable of 'The
Two Parrots and the Magpie' unnecessarily introduce words and,

what is worse, foreign phrases doing irreparable damage to our language because they deem it is so poor as to need to be dressed in foreign finery, so do they offend it who, at the opposite extreme, renew long-forgotten terms with no urgent motive, supposing it [the language] so poor as to need to take up again its once discarded finery." [23]

The last fable to be noted in this group recalls Iriarte's favorite theme of *utile dulci*. "The Gardener and His Master" (XLIX) concerns a foolish gardener who did not know how to mix practicality and pleasure—he was not able to use a fountain for both watering flowers and supplying a pond of fish with water. Iriarte writes at the end: "Though the maxim may be trite,/ Unless you have the skill,/ Taste and profit to unite,/ Lay by the author's quill." [24] Coming near the end of the collection, this fable sums up his attitude and underscores the purpose of his work in general.

The war between the Traditionalists and the Moderns gets its first treatment in fable IV, "The Drones and the Bee." The tone is muted, although the title immediately indicates the disparaging attitude of the writer toward those who only imitate and do not create. It is this sterile characteristic of the worst Traditionalists that Iriarte always condemned. We have seen it earlier regarding all noncreative literary activity. Here the fabulist is taking aim at those who refuse to admit invention and decry all newness, preferring to hide, because of their own inferiority, in the shadow of acceptable works from Antiquity: "How many there are, who their emptiness mask,/ By quoting wise words from the lips of the dead!/ But with all their pretence, did they ever, I ask,/ Produce any such from their own shallow head?" [25]

In another poem he more directly reprimands those who forsake their own literature for those foreign letters considered fashionable at the moment; Iriarte again follows a middle road in his attacks. This particular fable (XLI), "The Tea-Plant and Sage," deals with two plants often more appreciated by foreign nations than by their own. The sage says to the tea-plant:

> Good luck attend you to my native shore!
> For never yet was any nation known,
> But gold and praises will profusely pour
> On foreign products, while it slights its own."

> Now, I am sure that I can Spaniards show,
> Who will eternally be quoting
> Whole pages out of Tasso or Boileau;
> Yet never think or care to know
> What language Garcilaso wrote in.[26]

A further criticism is found in number XXIV, "The Thrush,
Parrot, and Magpie," where a thrush learns to speak from a parrot
(who had been originally taught by a man) and then teaches a
magpie. The resulting anarchy of speech can well be imagined.
To follow old models without invention on one's own part is bad
enough, but to do so through poor translations is even more
reprehensible. The translators themselves next come up for observation in XLIV, "The Sword and the Spit," where on the one
hand a spit is made into a sword and on the other, a priceless
sword is used to spit a hen:

> With equal knavery and stupidity,
> May not we charge these vile translators
> Who, with their works, in wretched rivalry,
> We see infesting all the world of Letters?
> One, with bad versions, famous writers fits—
> Thus turning noble swords to vulgar spits.
> Another clothes vile works in sounding words;
> Then, seeks to sell his spits for trusty swords.[27]

Iriarte continues his criticism in LVIII of translators and of
all those who refuse to base themselves on truth, who, in essence,
refuse to think for themselves. The fable is an admonition to both
Traditionalists and Moderns to follow the best of their beliefs and
not to shirk their responsibilities by following others' errors. The
poem is entitled, "The Watches." None of the watches agrees as
to the hour although one outspoken gentleman assures all that his
watch is always correct. Only one person, proficient in astronomy,
is able to determine the exact time. This disciple of the truth, the
sciences, and the rules concludes the fable: " 'To quote opinion
and authority/ Against the truth, if any one can see/ The use—
no point needs unsupported be./ For all can surely see, and must
admit, forsooth,/ Many opinions there may be—but only one is
truth!' " [28]

The theme of Traditionalism versus Modernism is referred

to quite directly near the end of the book. What Iriarte says only reaffirms his commitment to order, to reason, and to truth. He refuses to side with any faction that wanders off into extremes; a middle position is the best one, he reminds us. Reading what he says here (LXIII) and in other poems noted above, one sees that Iriarte cannot be categorized easily. The attempt to set him off in one camp, inimical to Spanish traditions, was made by Forner and most of Iriarte's other detractors. Their error can be nowhere better seen than in this fable called "The Connoisseurs." A group of wine connoisseurs can reach no decision about the best wine until one old gentleman arises and says:

"I tell you now, 'tis folly great
To think that every cask of wine,
Which on its head bears ancient date,
By age will mellow and refine.
Time cannot make the poor wine good;
If mean it was, in its first hour,
It will be washy still and crude,
In nothing changed, but turning sour.
Worth no jot more this hour, you know,
Than vinegar a century ago.
New wines, from time to time, there are,
Though some despise for being new,
Which very safely may compare
With any wines that ever grew. . . .
Bad wine I hold in low repute,
And ever do eschew.
But when 'tis good, I drain the flask;
And never vex myself to ask,
If it be old or new."
Many a learned bore
Keeps up a constant bother;
One praising ancient lore—
Modern alone, another.
By no such foolish question vexed,
I take the jolly toper's text;
The good, whate'er it is, I use;
The bad, without a word, refuse.[29]

As for the "mass man," Iriarte is not really concerned with him as a societal or cultural entity. Yet on several occasions he ven-

tures criticisms of that group of people exhibiting the *taste* of the
mass man—i.e., a taste that is indiscriminate, easily swayed or
perverted, and lacking in aesthetic authority. As a result of this
concept he declares himself against the idea of caprice or whim
so characteristic of this type of person. We cannot go so far as
to say that Iriarte in the *Fables* is openly antidemocratic in his
views of the common man. What he does feel and express agrees
completely with his inherent belief in the necessity for authority
and order. Since this belief is inherent in all really "enlightened"
people of the time (no matter how much they may have glorified
the idea of freedom and individuality), it is not surprising to find
it here. Beneath his diatribes against the tastes of the mass man,
there is still a respect for the man who remains true to himself
and does not bow to the dictates of a senseless authority.

This blind type of authority Iriarte never advocates. The most
direct of the fables in this grouping is number III, "The Bear, the
Monkey, and the Hog," whose theme is that a work is actually
condemned, not praised, when it is lauded by the ignorant. Iriarte
states in the moral at the end: "Authors, who seek a noble fame,/
Mark well the moral of my verse!/ That's bad which worthy
judges blame;/ What bad applaud, is worse." [30] It is a "mentality"
and not a man himself that Iriarte condemns. In fable XXVIII
noted earlier when Iriarte was condemning playwrights who
produce garbage for a public they think stupid and dull, he was
not criticizing the mass man but the attitude toward him. Here
in III he is criticizing an attitude usually associated with those
who are indiscriminate and therefore guilty of lowering the
levels of taste and quality. Another trait so common to the
mentality of the mass man is the one treated in fable IX, "The Ant
and the Flea." Its theme is that ignorant critics, in order not to
praise good works, strive to dismiss them as easy to produce,
knowing all along they themselves are incapable of creating anything comparable. The moral is stated at the beginning:

> A curious affectation some put on
> Of knowing everything they chance upon.
> Whatever matter they may hear or see,
> However new or excellent it may be,
> Of small account and easy always deem it,
> And never worthy of their praise esteem it.[31]

The result of the mentality criticized in this group of fables is the subject of number XVII, "The Linnet and the Swan." The swan's song is boasted of grandly, but when put to the test it is only a grotesque cackle: "Not strange, that empty reputation,/ Without, or skill or genius, at foundation,/ Should, upon trial, cheat the expectation!" [32] Much needless folly would cease in the area of letters if the mentality of the mass man were no longer heeded. Such is the message of the next fable. It is number XXXII, "The Fop and the Lady":

> A famous gallant, of Parisian renown . . .
> On the festival day of his lady love placed
> On his shoes two paltry buckles of tin;
> In order to show, by this frivolous whim,
> That he courted not fame, but that fame courted him.
> "What beautiful silver, so brilliant and gay!"
> Said the lady. "Huzza for the taste and the rule
> Of the master of fashion, the pride of our day!"
>
> Thus a volume of nonsense, or, I am a fool,
> The world will devour, if subscribed with the name
> Of a popular author, established in fame.[33]

The meaning and purpose of criticism are the subject of the last grouping of fables to be considered. The frustration and anger Iriarte himself felt at the hands of unjust and envious critics undoubtedly had much to do with the subject matter and tone of these particular poems. The first one below (XXXV), "The Silkworm and the Caterpillar," serves as a good introduction, for it sets forth the basic idea of this entire group—i.e., that envy and jealousy are often the foundations of criticism. When an old caterpillar decries the fine work of a silkworm, the fox spots the trouble immediately:

> "His mortified rancor he cannot control;
> He makes cocoons too, though they're worthless, we know."
>
> Laborious Genius! when, stung by the sneer
> Of the envious wretch who would rob you of glory,
> The loss of your well-deserved laurels you fear,
> Then take my advice and tell him this story.[34]

Fable XXXIV is even more blunt: "When envious detractors find/ In wise men's works, no welcome faults,/ They satisfy their spiteful mind/ By base and personal assaults." [35] Obviously reacting to the type of criticism that had been openly directed against him, Iriarte, having noted what this criticism is, states the dire consequences that come to this type of critic. In fable XXX, "The Author and the Rat," a rat keeps eating a scholar's library. Finally the author puts poison in his ink and abruptly ends the rat's career:

> Sarcastic said the Poet, thus relieved:
> "Let him, who gnaws too freely, have a care
> Lest his malicious insult prove a snare;
> And the impatient wight he seeks to bait,
> Should write him in corrosive sublimate." [36]

At the other extreme, Iriarte says that criticism should not be used as a vehicle to applaud a work unnecessarily. To promote this end is to pervert criticism as surely as to use it out of personal vindictiveness. Fable LVII, "The Lizards," deals with the harm resulting from lavishing too much attention on very insignificant objects:

> It is not worth the while to flatter
> The pride of writers we despise.
> 'Tis honoring too much the matter,
> To condescend to criticize.
> Their paltry trash in serious way
> To note—your pains will never pay.[37]

The last fable in the originally published collection fittingly stamps Iriarte's belief about criticism and, indeed, about moderation and adherence to rules—the basis of his book. "The Viper and the Leech" (LXVII) is deceivingly simple:

> "A strangely inconsistent crew!"
> Said the Viper to the simple Leech,
> "Men fly from me and seek for you;
> Although they get a bite from each."
> "All very true," the Leech replied,
> "But the two things are different quite.

I bite the sick, to give them aid;
To kill the sound and well, you bite."

Now, gentle reader, with you take
This counsel, as we part:
And always due distinction make,
If from the lash you smart.
Great is the difference between
Correction kind and malice keen.[38]

V *Popularity of the* Literary Fables

The diffusion of the *Literary Fables* has been notable. The editions in Spanish since 1782 have been numerous and they continue to be printed well into the present century. The translations have been equally remarkable and show the immediate popularity the poems gained outside Spain. The first translation was into Portuguese in 1796. The first English translation was in 1804. Some mention should be made here too of early advances in American letters in this regard—Devereux's translation (the one used in this chapter) was published in Boston in 1855. Interestingly, it appears not long after Ticknor's landmark work on Spanish literature. Italian translations appeared, but somewhat later than the first French one in 1801. A German translation was published in 1884.[39] In addition to these and other later ones not mentioned here, there were translations of individual fables. All this rather visible proof emphasizes the tremendous impact the *Fables* had on contemporary society. The polemics the work caused are also very immediate evidence of the way it aroused the public. Unfortunately, in its basic purpose of instructing, the work did not have such an obvious effect. Although it was, and still is, used as a textbook in grammar schools, it has been considered principally a significant Spanish contribution to the genre of the fable. This assertion is quite true but it indirectly denies the originality of the work. The *Literary Fables* are definitely unique in Spanish literature. They are the only Spanish Art of Poetry that really does "please while teaching." If such were not the case, the *Fables* would hardly have the popularity they still do. In addition to this more literary aspect of their value, they have a personal importance for Iriarte. They are the culmination of his literary career although they appear some nine years before his death. They come as a natural result of the teachings

The *Fábulas literarias*

imbibed in his youth and show in him that genius of originality that he always preached. The combination of originality and adherence to rules is nowhere else so evident or so fruitful in Spanish literature. By delineating so well the poet's tenets and even his own personal idiosyncrasies, the *Fables* should be considered one of the most significant, if not the most significant, works of the enlightened, Neoclassic spirit of the Spanish eighteenth century.

CHAPTER 4

Iriarte and the Theater

I The Translations

ONLY recently has the drama of Iriarte begun to receive any
serious consideration. To be sure, some of his contributions
to the theater were acknowledged much earlier. Leandro Fernández de Moratín was among the first to laud his success in the
late 1780's. In our own century Iriarte is treated, usually superficially, in studies of the Spanish eighteenth-century theater.
Hopefully this unnecessary disregard of Iriarte's important contributions to the regeneration of the Spanish drama is soon to
disappear. The valuable study by Subirá of a forgotten genre
that Iriarte introduced to Spain and a new edition [1] of Iriarte's
two most successful plays indicate a more profound evaluation of
Iriarte's efforts in the dramatic field. The fact is that Iriarte
deserves recognition for several reasons already seen in a more
general fashion in Chapter 1. He was among those who successfully translated plays in the early 1770's for presentation in the
Royal Theaters and was greatly responsible for making the French
Neoclassic drama more palatable to an admittedly hostile Spanish
audience. He also wrote an original play in the same year as
Nicolás Fernández de Moratín but was even more unlucky than
the latter because his was never even presented. There is good
reason to believe there was the animosity of some powerful enemies who prevented the public appearance of this play. Iriarte's
greatest success on the stage did not occur until the late 1780's
with the production of *El señorito mimado (The Pampered
Youth)*. This play, the first successful original Neoclassic comedy
in Spain, and its sequel *La señorita mal-criada (The Ill-Bred
Miss)* are of extreme value in any consideration of the fate of
Spanish Neoclassic drama. Also the production of a short play
Guzmán el bueno (Guzmán, The Good) several years later grants
Iriarte renown as both an innovator and creator that has been
for the most part unjustly denied him.

Iriarte and the Theater

Some notice was given in the first chapter to the Iriartes' participation in the renovation of the theater that actively began under Aranda in the 1760's. Bernardo de Iriarte wrote a plan of reform in 1767 that had to do with the more visible aspects of dramatic production. Others had made earlier efforts in the same direction but with less success. In 1765 the *autos sacramentales* had been forbidden. Even earlier Clavijo y Fajardo had founded his newspaper *El pensador* in order to attack the contemporary state of the Spanish theater. He was joined in his efforts by Nifo, and between the two of them the attack began to reach a wider audience. Heretofore, the criticism had mainly circulated among a limited number of scholars. A great debt is owed to Clavijo and to Nifo for their efforts in spreading the desire for a change in the climate of the theater. To Bernardo de Iriarte is owed appreciation for setting up a set of criteria for judging whether plays were acceptable or not and for providing some seventy plays (out of approximately six hundred chosen principally from seventeenth-century Spanish dramatists) considered presentable on the stage. He felt that obscenity or baseness in any form was not to be permitted. Comedies were to be changed so as to meet the demand for verisimilitude. The unities were to be observed. He even went so far as to demand the rejection once and for all of those plays containing magic, friars, or devils—in short, all those artifices of extravagance that the more vociferous elements of the audience demanded. It was essentially the propensity to applaud the superficial, banal qualities of a work that most annoyed the Spanish Neoclassicists. Iriarte further suggested that to obtain really good plays, writers should translate the best of the French and Italian dramas. Naturally such a recommendation did little to placate the enemies of these much-needed reforms. To put the reforms into effect Aranda in the late 1760's began erecting a theater in each of the principal royal residences. He thought it best to begin changing the climate at its point of least resistance. Had these new measures been better and more efficiently advertised, they would probably have met with a more decent reception from the general public. But because of the bluntness with which most new ideas in any field were introduced (witness the reforms and the resultant *motín de Esquilache* in the 1760's),[2] the public refused to accept them and, more often than not, violently attacked them.

From approximately 1768 on, a great many plays were translated and produced on the Spanish stage, but to a select minority. They all conformed to the idea of taste demanded by Bernardo de Iriarte. Most of them were in prose because it was thought they would in this way appear more realistic. The plays translated by Tomás de Iriarte were numerous and in general were in prose. Two of them (only these two will be treated here) were written in verse and they are the ones included in the two collections of his complete works. He makes a statement about his method of translation that is of interest because it indicates the basic ambience sought by all the translators. The idea was not so much to give a close translation but an adaptation of the original to the Spanish scene. It was this spirit that Bernardo de Iriarte most certainly had in mind when he recommended the translation of French and Italian works. Tomás de Iriarte writes in the short prologue to his translations: "[the author] translated them without sticking too closely to the originals, and adding or taking out what seemed to him appropriate because both the differences of our customs and language and the determination to not allow any maxim or expression that might be offensive demanded it." [3]

The first of the two plays is a comedy in five acts by Destouches called *El filósofo casado o el marido avergonzado de serlo (The Married Philosopher or The Husband Ashamed of Being So)*. It is a clever presentation of the dilemma of a young man, Don Carlos, who professes to be led on by great ideals but who balks when he feels the source of his finances, his uncle, may not approve of his actions. In such a case he resorts to deception, somehow making deceit a perfect companion for his idealism. Don Carlos has been married for two years but refuses to let his deceit be known. At first he tells us it is from fear of hurting his father, but we soon discover it is from the fear of being disinherited by his wealthy uncle. The whole play centers around whether or not his situation will be publicized.

Entering the plot to keep it lively by adding new twists is his friend the Marquis of Rueda, who falls in love with Carlos' wife Jacinta. In addition to worrying about the cessation of his uncle's assistance, Carlos now has to worry about his friend's discovering his situation and almost certainly the friend's cruel mockery of the antimarital diatribes previously delivered by Carlos at every turn. But neither can Carlos ask the Marquis to stop his attentions to the former's wife without telling him why. Fortunately the wife is sensible and cools the Marquis's ardor herself. In fact, Jacinta is about the only one in the play who displays some degree of common sense. Her sister Rosa is a completely spoiled young woman courted by Luis, Carlos' friend and confidant. It is she who in her blunt way finally insures the secret will be known by telling it to some of her friends. The uncle in the meantime arrives and declares that Carlos will marry his stepdaughter or else lose the promised inheritance. Carlos' father, who is also present, is the typical eighteenth-century *bonhomme* who has lost his fortune because of a question of honor. Carlos at last tells him of his marriage and the kindly old gentleman seeks to help him. But at the end it is Carlos himself who decides to be truly a *philosophe* and stand up for what he believes: when the uncle threatens to take him to court and send Jacinta to a convent, Carlos renounces his greed and declares he will have Jacinta rather than all the money in the world. Naturally, the point of the drama being made, all comes to a rapid and happy conclusion. The Marquis marries the stepdaughter; Luis marries Rosa; and Carlos and Jacinta can now live contentedly together in public.

The second drama, a tragedy in five acts by Voltaire, is called *El huérfano de la China (The Chinese Orphan).* It is one of those plays so often set either in Ancient Greece or Rome or, as in this case, in the Orient. Although it thus has an exotic setting, its purpose is to present a moral dilemma that is to be considered both Western and contemporary. Genghis Khan has conquered China and killed the Emperor and all his family except one last male child who is hidden away by Zamtí, a mandarin prince, and his wife Idame. Zamtí had promised the Emperor he would save the child. The conflict of the play occurs when the conqueror demands the child be found and killed. Zamtí, knowing the hiding place will soon be discovered, delivers up his own son to almost certain death rather than betray his word to his sovereign. Idame, overcome with grief, seeks to save both children, an act in which she rather miraculously succeeds for a while. She is able to talk with the conqueror who years before, as an unknown and a commoner, had loved her. Finally, he demands that she either give herself to him thus freeing her husband and the heir to the throne or he will have them both killed. Idame is placed in the unhappy position of either indirectly killing her husband or of destroying his honor. In the final act she decides to have Zamtí stab her to death, thus freeing them all. She and her husband have done all they can to maintain his pledge and their own integrity. But at that precise moment Genghis Khan enters saying their virtue has changed him from a barbarian to a civilized man, from a conqueror to a king. He will make Zamtí the principal interpreter and administrator of law and will himself place the family, including the heir to the throne, under his protection.

For Iriarte, and those of like mind, both plays were good examples of what it was thought the new drama should be in Spain. The plots are relatively simple, they teach a moral lesson, and the first of the two at least entertains while the latter is supposed to uplift the mind and the spirit. Both plays are a far cry from the exaggerated, syrupy, even ludicrously weak fare that the public was usually provided, this fare being poor productions of the worst Golden Age dramas or very bad imitations of them. This latter theater was a source of entertainment and was not necessarily supposed to teach or to mold the audience's thinking. At this time the drama in general in Spain was receiving much the same kind of criticism that the books of chivalry had received some two hundred years before—i.e., that it was empty, debased and debasing, and served no visibly useful purpose. The criticism was in its turn exaggerated, but most of it needed saying and the Neoclassicists were the first really to try to remedy the deplorable state of the national drama. Both during and after their attempts to insert a note of sanity into the theater, they were attacked for being sterile, dry, and dull; and in many instances this criticism was justified. Nevertheless, if their direction of change was toward a too severe simplicity, it is not unexpected and should not be unduly faulted, for a reaction to one extreme usually results in a shift to the opposite extreme.

The two translations by Iriarte are valuable because in them, and more specifically in the way Iriarte handles the language and the creation of ambience, the Neoclassic artist is seen in his most essential attitude. He is seeking to present very simply a moral dilemma in which the protagonist is rewarded or punished according to how he reacts to the problem that confronts him. In the case of the comedy, the reader is taught and entertained. In the tragedy he is to be completely transported from the physical world of the moment to one more noble and ethereal. Both types thus move the viewer, changing him in some way hopefully, but by no means does he merely have his senses caressed. The idea is to enrich the audience's experience, to improve its vision and understanding. This essentially Classical attitude is expectedly inherent in the Neoclassicist. It is also perhaps one of the main reasons for his considering himself too frequently an infallible messiah and, as a result, is what usually involved him in fruitless, endless polemics.

Iriarte, in converting these plays into Spanish, produced a form and tone that make them seem entirely native. Even in *The Chinese Orphan* the atmosphere is never Oriental, but Western. The moral values so highly proclaimed are those long associated with the Spanish mentality. Zamtí remains true to his integrity or concept of personal honor in the face of all odds. Idame is the strong, serious Spanish heroine who recalls in a minor key Laurencia in *Fuente Ovejuna*. The projection of a Spanish type is even more evident in the personage of the father in *The Married Philosopher*. Don Esteban is the epitome of the stereotyped noble Spanish gentleman who maintains his sense of nobility in the face of overwhelming odds. It is nothing to him that he has lost his financial stability so long as he has retained his honor. These characters and their qualities are not original with Iriarte; yet it is he who acclimates them to the Spanish scene and removes any feeling of foreignness they might have had.

II Hacer que hacemos *and* Los literatos en cuaresma

At the same time that he was making his translations, Iriarte wrote his first original drama called *Hacer que hacemos (The Busybody)*. It was a comedy in three acts and in verse and was published in 1770 under the anagram of Tirso Imareta. The author's purpose in writing was to ridicule a type of person, the busybody of the title. He thought that this type would be of greater interest to an audience than some other kinds of persons because the very nature of the type would cause a variety of diverting scenes. Iriarte's aim was to present a play that conformed to the Classical rules and, naturally, taught a moral lesson. The plot centers around Don Gil, who is to marry Doña Elvira. Yet throughout the play Don Gil appears to have so many other things to do that he has little time for what should be his one goal at this moment. He runs hither and yon throughout the duration of the play, forever talking about all he must do but never really accomplishing anything. Most of the things he is involved in are of little consequence anyway. So burdened is he with his responsibilities, however, that he does not permit himself time to talk to Doña Elvira or even to her father who comes to discuss the marriage. In the end he never marries Doña Elvira. There is a secondary plot in the love affair of Don Miguel and Doña Vicenta, the sister of Don Gil.

The purpose of Iriarte's play is to condemn Don Gil and what he represents. It might be added here that this type of individual was one that always annoyed Iriarte and was the subject of numerous poems and frequent references in his essays. The problem with the play is that Don Gil never really becomes a person. The fact is that Iriarte makes no real attempt to have the character realize how stupid and ridiculous he actually is. Without this self-knowledge there is quite expectedly little attempt at repentance on Don Gil's part. In this failure to have the protagonist truly realize and then remedy his faults, Iriarte lessens the possibility of his protagonist's and thus his drama's being taken seriously. Unfortunately, the play comes across simply as an empty shell with no real interior. Probably as a result, most critics have sought out the principal merit of the work in its brilliant dialogue and versification, two aspects that do deserve commendation. Even though these are laudable attributes, oddly enough they may have had an adverse effect on the criticism of Iriarte in general. From about this time on, i.e., the 1770's, critics have tended to see in him the gifted stylist but rarely the gifted creator, except, of course, for a work like the *Literary Fables*. This is an unjust view of him but it is one that has been popular until recently. Such a trend in the criticism about the writer could very well have had its beginnings here in this ill-fated play. The play was never produced and had only the one printing in 1770 since it was not included in either the 1787 or 1805 collections of Iriarte's work. Yet it should be remembered that the play was original, that it came when the writer was still very young, and that its fate was not much worse than that of the often-mentioned *Hormesinda* by Moratín which appeared in the same year.

Iriarte believed that his play was not produced principally because of the influence of Ramón de la Cruz, who was antagonistic to the dictates of Neoclassicism although he at one time had

some association with that school. It is conceivable that Ramón
de la Cruz did exercise his power to thwart Iriarte's plans, but
concrete proof is somewhat difficult to find. It is known that he
did bait the Neoclassicists whenever an occasion presented itself,
usually taunting them with their lack of popular success. If he did
indeed ruin some of the opportunities for their acceptance, his
taunts were doubly venomous and unforgivable. Whatever his
true feeling toward Iriarte was at that time, Iriarte wrote his first
successful essay directed at the older man. *Los literatos en
cuaresma (Writers in Lent)*, published in 1773 and probably inspired by Cadalso's recent, successful *Los eruditos a la violeta
(The Superficial Erudites)*, is both a defense of the Neoclassicists
and indirectly a goad to prod them to achieve more.

The structure of *Writers in Lent* is a kind of dialogue much
in the form of the *tertulia* or salon which was so popular particularly at that time. The group sets aside six themes for discussion that are taken up on the six Sundays of Lent. Iriarte's
points, expressed in what would become his normal, cogent prose
style, are numerous. He states that drama in Spain can still not
be distinguished from novels and chronicles. He laments the fact
that Spaniards still argue about the unities while other nations
have passed beyond this primitive level and are using them truly
to improve the theater. He goes into some detail about the unities,
providing exaggerated examples to get his points across. He ad-
vises against believing that the mere observance of the unities
is enough to make a drama perfect. There are other requirements
that are essential as well and without which no play can succeed.
These include cleverness in plot, a certain measure of realism,
variety in dialogue, purity of style, appropriateness of theme,
and finally that quality most difficult to achieve—the arousal of
interest. After all these considerations, there is still another, over
which he has no real control, but which can mean the downfall
of any author. This last consideration is the makeup of the audience. Its level of quality and education can either make or break
a play. Iriarte is perhaps thinking of his own misfortune with
The Busybody. He particularly criticizes that public which is so
attuned to the abuses of the popular drama of the day that it
cannot—or does not wish to—appreciate a play that follows the
Classic rules. He then elucidates the theater as he thinks it should
be. Recognizing the good the Spanish government has attempted

to do in the theater, especially under the guidance of Aranda, Iriarte feels confident Spanish drama will be improved by adopting what is good in the theater of other nations while not negating the good features of its own. This idea is essentially that held by all the Spanish Neoclassic dramatists. He believes further that the only thing the new artists need to make them more productive and more successful is some gesture of approval from the public. He here launches into a defense of the art of translation, probably because at this time so much of his work was precisely in that area. The art of translating is not generally understood according to Iriarte. The worth of translations should be assessed only by those who appreciate the difficulties involved and who understand the service translations can render to the public.

These and other observations compose *Writers in Lent*. It is certainly a commendable work and provides a good defense of the Neoclassicists while not overpraising them. Indeed it is in the characteristic restraint of Iriarte that the treatise is valuable because the author is seeking in a somewhat indirect way to urge his compatriots on. He is quite worried about the lack of any really visible successes, especially on the stage, on the part of his fellow Neoclassicists. The work then has a tone and direction that are too often missed by readers and the critics in particular. It is more than just a defense of the writer himself; it is more than a veiled diatribe against Ramón de la Cruz and all that he represented on the contemporary Spanish stage; and finally, it is more than a chauvinistic defense of his friends. The work is an attempt to summarize in a cogent fashion what had occurred and was occurring on the literary scene. It strives to point out what is good and bad in that area and suggest where writers must direct themselves. Because of the temperament of the times critics chose to overlook the valid criticism and worthy suggestions, preferring to pounce upon the more sensational *ad hominem* attacks that could be found since, just as in our tabloids of today, these were felt to be more enjoyed by the public. As a result the rather unusual and intriguing format of the work and, above all, its ideas have been overlooked ever since. The public, when it has examined the essay, has tended to remember only the qualities historically applicable to the times. The outcome was much the same as with that of *Give and Take* where the personal attacks on Sedano were emphasized by the critics. The valuable contributions of Iriarte to literary criticism were forgotten in preference to the almost prurient interest of the public in more superficial, albeit entertaining, aspects of the work.

III   *Ultimate Success in the Theater*

After the near fiasco of *The Busybody*, Iriarte made no serious attempts to write for the stage for several years. It was during this time, as we have seen, that he produced his more memorable works such as the *Literary Fables*. However, always in the back of his mind was the desire to write a play in which he would put into effect his ideas about what the new theater should be. Perhaps the worst defect of *The Busybody* was that the central character did not ring true, either as a human being or even as a type. It was to correct this defect that Iriarte began to direct himself. It was taken for granted that a play would have to teach, to have a moral. The greatest difficulty would be solely to present a type who in his general makeup would be more believable and therefore more acceptable to the public. Iriarte eliminated this difficulty by choosing a type that was easily recognizable in Madrid, or anywhere else, for that matter: the pampered, spoiled offspring of a too indulgent mother. The play *El señorito mimado* *(The Pampered Youth)* was written in the early 1780's and was printed in Volume IV of the complete works in 1787. With the favorable reaction the printed version received, Iriarte decided to have the play produced. It appeared in September, 1788, to a thunderous reception. In the introduction to his own plays Moratín wrote of this drama:

Not without some difficulty did the above-mentioned Iriarte succeed in bringing to the stage in 1788 his comedy *The Pampered Youth*, which, quite well presented by the company of Martínez, won the applause of the audience, with special attention to its moral objective, its plan, its characters, and the facility and purity of its versification and style. Perhaps it did merit the censure by those who noted its lack of dramatic movement, of levity, and of comic relief; but these defects are easily overwhelmed by the many qualities that made it estimable in both its stage presentation and its printed form. *If one is to cite the first original comedy in the Spanish theater written according to the rules dictated by philosophy and good criticism, it is this one* [italics mine].[4]

The drama, written in verse and in three acts, illustrates what happens to a dissipated, naïve youth. Oddly, however, it does not condemn the young man so much as it does his mother. The play begins as Don Christóval audits the accounts left by his profligate nephew, Don Mariano, the protagonist of the drama. Don Christóval becomes increasingly angry with his findings and begins to criticize Doña Dominga, Mariano's too lenient mother. The fact is that Christóval has just returned from the New World and is horrified at the lack of discipline so blatantly exhibited by his young relative. Doña Dominga, being the rather ingenuous but well-meaning person she is, tries to soothe her brother-in-law and tells him not to fault her son. He retorts that it is she who is really to blame for the shameful condition of Mariano: "Yes, against you I cry out. What an upbringing! Now we shall all have to pay for the damage when it is really no one's fault but your own. Your easy-going disposition, your blind love for your son, your indulgence. . . . In short, I return from my trip quite content and what do I find but that my nephew will soon be twenty years old and does not even know how to make the sign of the cross . . . that he is stubborn, effeminate, insolent. . . ." [5]

This, then, is the hero of the play—and it really seems to bother his mother very little. Pantoja, the faithful family servant who is much maligned by his mistress, enters to add further to Don Christóval's list of his young master's deficiencies. As soon as Christóval had left for America, the tutor had been dismissed and Mariano's education virtually was nonexistent thereafter. In addition he has taken up with a certain Doña Mónica and her brother-in-law Don Tadeo, both of whom Doña Dominga has accepted as reliable people. Doña Dominga then relates that what Mariano really needs is a young, understanding wife, and even this last whim she has been able to provide for her son. Visiting her now, she informs us, are an old family friend Don Alfonso and his daughter, Doña Flora. The marriage of the latter and Mariano is fairly assured, asserts Doña Dominga. At this moment Don Alfonso enters and after some idle conversation, he begins to tell what he has heard of his proposed son-in-law and that he now doubts the wisdom of the marriage.

At this point Don Fausto enters. He is a friend of Mariano and has been involved in a lawsuit with Don Alfonso. It was an unwanted legal entanglement inherited from other members of his family, and Fausto, because of a sense of familial duty, felt obliged to see the matter through. He has just this day lost the case to Don Alfonso, but his admiration for the old gentleman whose integrity he has long known and respected is such, however, that he is not angry. Besides, he is in love with Flora. Later he meets Mariano, who first arrives on the stage looking just like the pleasant fop one would expect from the descriptions of him by the various personages up to this point. He comes out poorly in contrast with Fausto, who incarnates stability, reason, and graciousness. In the following scenes Doña Flora appears, and Fausto presents her the portrait of herself she had given to Mariano but which he had left in the hands of Doña Mónica. The latter had sold it to Fausto and he now returns it to its original owner, indirectly making sure she understands the circuitous route her picture has traveled.

As Act Two begins, Mariano's machinations are beginning to catch up with him. He is having an argument with his mother concerning money. Yet she persists in her lenient attitude, even when she discovers that he has pawned a diamond ring of hers he was to have given to Flora. Dominga is actually angry with Pantoja when she discovers it is he who redeemed the ring and has thus saved it from being lost to the family forever. She considers his action arrogant. Mariano next finds himself in trouble with Flora who, angry over the incident concerning her portrait, induces him to show her that he still has the portrait. He thinks he does have her picture and gives her a picture which, unfortunately for him, is one Mónica had substituted for Flora's. Mónica had kept the original picture and sold it to Fausto as we have already seen. Flora is angry and now fully disillusioned. Mariano realizes too that Mónica is trying to snare him completely in her web, for we have been given hints enough by now to know that Mónica is evidently not the grand lady she has portrayed herself to be.

In the following scenes Christóval tells Doña Dominga what he has seen in Mónica's house which is more a gambling den than anything else. Dominga refuses to believe him and sides with Mónica, who now appears on the stage to proclaim her indignation at Christóval's entrance into her house. She then says that she has a promise of marriage signed by Mariano and she intends to hold him to it or otherwise there will be trouble. Confronted with his deed, Mariano says he signed the promise while inebriated and at the instigation of his friends. The wily brother-in-law was the one who drew up the unfortunate document. Don Alfonso appears and comically unmasks Mónica who it seems is the lowly daughter of an Andalusian innkeeper. She has been constantly in trouble with the law. Now at a loss as to what to do at these unhappy revelations, Mónica successfully pretends to faint.

The third act is opened by Mónica's trying to reassure Mariano that she really is all she has claimed to be and that it is his uncle and Don Alfonso who lie. She talks him into coming to her house that night, bringing the money his mother has given him to retrieve the diamond ring. As she leaves, Mónica hands him a note which reveals it is supposedly from Fausto to Flora telling her how happy he is that she at last has seen the true side of Mariano. Of course this letter is false since it is the handiwork of Tadeo and is part of his and Mónica's plan to get the unsuspecting Mariano more involved with them. When Mariano abruptly confronts Fausto with the letter and berates him in an ungentlemanly manner, Fausto challenges him. The idea of a duel is not at all to Mariano's liking and he runs to his uncle to get him out of the situation he has forced himself into. In scene six there is a change in tone and pace when Fausto, with Flora, comes to ask Alfonso for his daughter in marriage. Flora quite readily admits her folly in ever trusting Mariano. In succeeding scenes, Mariano goes to Mónica's house although Christóval has expressly forbidden him to do so.

Doña Dominga is quite upset when she finds out from Pantoja what has happened. However, she hopes to remedy the sad state of affairs when a notary appears saying that for a price Mónica will renounce all claims she has on Mariano. Dominga is overjoyed and quickly gives him the money. Quite soon she discovers she too has been duped, for the notary was none other than Tadeo. As the act draws to an end Christóval announces that Mónica and her confederates have been taken into custody. Dominga is relieved, only to be again disheartened because Mariano too has been apprehended and then sentenced to banishment from the capital for two years. Christóval announces his nephew will be sent to Valencia where a friend hopefully will be able to begin changing Mariano's ways: "Begin to live again from this point on. You fully realize the state into which laziness, ignorance, and the habits of a bad education have catapulted you." [6] Mariano still cannot believe he has lost until he is bluntly told that Flora is no longer his. At this news he is finally undone. His uncle takes the reaction as a promising sign, however: "What? You become confused? That is not a bad sign. With that, if you some day have children, you can cite them this example, and if you do not better instruct them, what is happening to you today will also happen to them." [7]

Concurrent with the success of *The Pampered Youth,* Iriarte published another play in 1788 which was not produced until 1791. It too is in three acts and in verse, and is a variation on the theme of the above. Here it is the father who unduly pampers his willful daughter. *La señorita mal-criada (The Ill-Bred Miss)* opens with great activity as Tío Pedro, the majordomo, drives away some musicians who are destroying the peace of his domain. Bártolo, the likable but meddlesome gardener, informs him, however, that the musicians have been invited since it is to be a day of celebration. There then follows an introduction of all the characters with brief résumés of their personalities. This novel procedure is accomplished in an amusing and psychologically penetrating manner through the rustic language of the two servants. Tío Pedro is much more reserved and severe in his delivery while Bártolo is earthy and blunt.

The stage is now set for us to meet the characters in person. This artful device thus has the useful advantage of enhancing and expanding the unity of time since we know the characters rather well even before they appear. Don Gonzalo, the father of Pepita the protagonist and the owner of the country house where the action takes place, comes out dressed as a hunter. We learn that he has walked out early from his house in Madrid. Belying his dress and his walk, we soon discover that he is a lover of society and the high life. He is a man who prefers not to curtail or restrain his enjoyment of physical pleasures. Such a characteristic has colored all aspects of his life and has ultimately permitted him to spoil his daughter to an incredible degree. Because of her father's indulgence Pepita has no sense of obligation to anyone or anything but herself. It is about this particular point that Gonzalo's sister and brother-in-law have not been on speaking terms with him for several years. Yet today the celebration is occurring because all have forgiven each other. Don Basilio and

Doña Clara now arrive, the picture of logic and good taste. They are accompanied by Don Eugenio, a wealthy friend of Don Gonzalo, who seeks to marry Pepita although she cares little for him. They all talk about the deplorable state of Pepita's character. She is a vacuous and socially inept young lady.

As we have already noted, basically Pepita's imperfections are due to Gonzalo's lack of supervision. This, the main theme of the play, has a quite obvious parallel to that of *The Pampered Youth*. But Pepita's gaucherie is at this time more attributable to Doña Ambrosia, a young widow befriended by Gonzalo and the intimate friend and mentor of Pepita. Ambrosia was married to a wealthy merchant until he was swindled by a supposed friend who fled the country after his deed. Within a week of his disgrace her husband died, and his nephew Carlos has been searching for the culprit for four years. Carlos' imminent return is mentioned in passing by Gonzalo. In scene five Pepita and Ambrosia enter, and we indirectly see the clash between the former and her aunt, Clara. The clash represents a part of the theme of the play, the confrontation between sybaritic pleasure and good manners. Rather than greet her guests, Pepita elects to applaud the musicians who have begun to play at her entrance and begs them to continue. Clara reprimands her and in a fit of pique Pepita dismisses the entertainers and then refuses to do whatever the guests prefer. In scene seven the Marquis who also wants to marry Pepita, but only for purposes of financial gain, appears and we see immediately the devious, foppish creature he is. He and Ambrosia plan to discredit Eugenio by leaving a forged letter in the latter's pocket. This feat they achieve by drawing Eugenio into a conversation about a supposedly anonymous sonnet actually written by the Marquis. The sonnet is atrocious, full of many of the defects of the Frenchified style in Spanish, and Don Eugenio bluntly says so. In the final scene of the act Don Basilio restates the problem to be faced in the play: what to do about Pepita who is obviously headed for a fall if she continues in her self-centered ways and marries the Marquis. Thus, in structure, the first act has neatly presented us the characters and their idiosyncrasies and the problems they, and we, face in the drama.

The second act further entangles the action. Tío Pedro delivers a letter to Gonzalo wherein he is told that a business venture of Eugenio's in which Gonzalo heavily invested is failing. The letter is false and had been sent earlier by Ambrosia and the Marquis. Eugenio in the following scenes gives some opinions concerning women to Pepita since she has asked what he thinks the role of women should be in society. He talks to her personally and criticizes her empty, coquettish existence, telling her she will end up unmarried, unloved, and totally embittered against mankind. He gives her some pertinent advice that still rings quite true:

DON EUGENIO: . . . in this small world we are all part of each other. I would hope you would come to abhor that tyrannical system where . . . men consider women born only to be their slaves. . . .
DOÑA PEPITA: . . . [otherwise] they will call me a scholar.
DON EUGENIO: Only those who refuse to admit that there are tasks no less appropriate for one sex than for the other will think that way. Who does not admire a woman who unites in her natural brilliance the useful knowledge of history, of ethics, of geography, of languages. . . ? [8]

Pepita is scornful of all he says and she later agrees with Ambrosia's negative approach to men and to the world. We are returned to the plot abruptly after Ambrosia's long discourse on how women must act around men when Gonzalo confronts Eugenio with the above-noted letter. Eugenio protests and in his innocence accidentally pulls out the letter earlier inserted in his pocket by Ambrosia. Since it is in the same handwriting as the one delivered by Tío Pedro, Gonzalo refuses to believe his protestations. Soon Pepita joins the forces against Eugenio and tells her father she is certain that the relationship between her aunt and Eugenio is more than merely a friendly one since he has several gifts from Doña Clara. The plot is further complicated by Ambrosia's open courting of Gonzalo, who quite eagerly receives her advances. At the end of Act Two the two camps of personages and philosophies are solidly arrayed against each other.

At the beginning of Act Three Doña Clara states she would much prefer to escape the confusion that is increasing on all sides. Nevertheless, she is determined to stay and see that reason triumphs in Gonzalo's household. In the meantime Bártolo tells Basilio that he saw Ambrosia place the false letter in Eugenio's coat pocket. Later among some papers of the Marquis the rough draft of the letter is discovered. The so-called suspicious gifts of Clara to Eugenio are explained and Clara delivers some harsh statements about the stupidity of those who believe gossip about a man and a woman being lovers when they are in truth only friends. The Marquis's unfortunate letter is shown to Gonzalo at about the same time that Carlos, the nephew of Ambrosia's former husband, appears and dramatically exposes the Marquis as the "murderer" of her husband. Both Ambrosia and Pepita are by this time utterly humiliated in their mutual folly, and reason completely triumphs over self-indulgence when Gonzalo woefully declares in his final speech: ". . . henceforth I shall learn to be more cautious; and let other careless fathers learn from my example." [9]

A very short one-act play in prose, evidently written sometime in the early 1780's, which was presented with success several times during the writer's life is *La librería (The Bookstore)*. It is an excellent example of the popular genre, the *sainete*. First and most important is that it has a moral, a thing so desired by the Neoclassicists. There is music but in sensible quantities so that the flow of the play is not disturbed. The characters are well developed; in short, taste has been observed in every possible way. The play, funny and quick-paced, basically concerns who will marry Feliciana, the niece of the Bookseller. His wife Nicolasa is determined that it will not be Fermín, the shop's apprentice who is in love with Feliciana. The drama is a tour de force essentially maintained by three outrageous persons: Don Silvestre, who delights in his own extravagant conversation; Don Roque, a rather outlandish poet; and Don Isidro, who is more fond of gambling than anything else. The play like so many of this type begins with music, accompanying Feliciana's lament of the loss of the person she most loves. We soon discover that Fermín is from a good, educated family but in bad financial straits at the moment. He has taught Feliciana a great deal since beginning to work in the bookstore. The theme of the unnecessary illiteracy of women already noted in *The Ill-Bred Miss* is again presented. Fermín was dismissed from the store because Nicolasa could not bear to think that he might be in love with her niece. Her jealousy of her niece is almost as great as her determination to oppose her husband in every way possible. When the Bookseller promises Feliciana's hand in marriage to Don Silvestre and Nicolasa promises her to Don Isidro, confusion is bound to re-

sult. After a scene of complete chaos—which must be even fun-
nier when seen on the stage—the two would-be suitors accompanied by Don Roque stalk out leaving Fermín the prize he
has sought. For once the Bookseller stands up to his wife who
meekly submits. Feliciana declares she now can sing happily and
the Bookseller concurs: "Whenever you wish, sing; for I would
much rather see my store peaceful and happy, than overwhelmed
with the cries and arguments of those people." [10]

The last two plays written by Iriarte were composed in 1790.
The longer one in three acts and written in verse is called *El don
de gentes o La habanera (Winning Ways or The Girl From Havana)*. The plot, which attempts to portray what the perfect
woman should be, is quite simple. Rosalía, young and of noble
birth, is shipwrecked while traveling from Havana to Spain. Her
uncle is drowned, leaving her destitute. Unable to reach her
cousin to whose house she was being sent in the beginning, she
becomes a servant in the house of Don Alberto. Everyone is immediately captivated by her except Doña Elena, a young widow,
who it seems is bitter and unkind to almost everyone. Soon both
Don Alberto and his son Leandro are seeking the hand of Rosalía.
Gutiérrez, the worthy servant, also is charmed by her. Finally it
is Leandro who wins her. This occurs to the accompanying revela-
tion of who Rosalía is. All are happy at the solution. Throughout
the play Rosalía is portrayed as the perfect young lady scorning
the warmth and friendship of no one and showing herself to be
that ideally sensible young woman that Iriarte sketched partially
in *The Ill-Bred Miss* and *The Bookstore*. The play was meant to
be followed by a shorter comic piece entitled *Donde menos se
piensa salta la liebre (It Would Happen Where Least Expected)*.
Its main attribute is its excellent depiction of certain types. It is
interesting to note too that one of its characters, the Licentiate,
one of the most exuberant and lovable of pedants, antecedes Don
Eleuterio in Moratín's *La comedia nueva (The New Comedy)*. The
title alone of his magnum opus is enough to convulse an audience.

These résumés, albeit brief, give some idea as to what the content of Iriarte's plays is like. To two of them more attention was
given because it is these two that received more public notice and
they therefore deserve a bit more attention here. But leaving all
this aside, we are immediately impressed by the plays, not only
separately but as a whole, for one particular reason: they inculcate

some moral. Their tone, whether they have few or many comic touches, is one that elevates, that uplifts the public mind and spirit. It is that characteristic inherent in all Neoclassic artists. But more important for us is that it is the trait most often found in Iriarte's writing. It was first most soundly evident in his choice of a work to translate from Latin. The *Poetics* of Horace we discovered was a natural choice for Iriarte because it contained those tenets that he held most dear. The theme of *utile dulci* comes across in all these plays then as a resultant attribute of Iriarte's concept of the purpose of writing. The tremendously important thing about Iriarte's plays is that that concept does not overwhelm the works themselves, which is not ordinarily the case in other Neoclassic plays up to the time of Moratín's success in the 1790's. Iriarte's works have a point to make, but the theme does not become the blatantly obvious preoccupation of the writer. Iriarte has a good feeling for what is dramatic that many of his contemporaries lacked. He is able to employ a certain balancing of the elements of drama that seemed to escape others. So many Neoclassic dramatists sought to avoid the abhorred excesses of the Traditionalist school so much that they failed to include any sense of levity at all. Iriarte is once again able to travel the middle of the road and falls into the excesses of neither school, although he is of course a Neoclassicist by conviction.

This characteristic of Iriarte's writing, that is, his sense of balance, is probably best seen in the treatment of the characters in the plays. In *The Pampered Youth* three characters stand out, but in different ways. The uncle is perhaps the weakest as a real person, but he represents responsibility and personal integrity, and to make such attributes believable it is often difficult to have the possessor of them seem totally real at the same time. It is rather the mother and the son, and this in spite of his being admittedly a type, who come across most forcefully as real people. Iriarte has obviously learned a lesson from *The Busybody* in his creation of Mariano. He is a type that all too often abounds, but he is believable precisely because of his recognizability. His being a type does not negate his human reality. The mother in her rather pathetic way is also real and at the end especially she awakens our sympathy. All three characters arouse our sympathy, each in his own way and at different places in the drama. It does seem odd that an excessively upright, mature man, a weak, vacillating mother, and a foppish, boorish son could arouse our emotions, but they do.

In *The Ill-Bred Miss* there is also a nucleus of characters to whom we react positively. Clara and Gonzalo, sister and brother but temperamentally as opposite. as can be imagined, are excellently portrayed. Their personalities and the clash of their philosophies draw us to them. Again they come across as living human beings and not as cardboard figures. The same is true of Ambrosia, the widow. She is sly and cruel although seemingly vapid. Iriarte credits much of her devious behavior to the ill treatment the world has afforded her. He ingeniously attracts us in her creation while at the same time superficially he repels us. Finally in this particular drama the servants are extremely important. One, Bártolo, provides spontaneity, but it is a sensible and purposeful spontaneity as opposed to Pepita's, which is more a brand of self-indulgence. The other servant, Tío Pedro, is Bártolo's opposite; he provides a serious tone to counterbalance the scene. Taken all together, we have a kind of seesaw effect of human emotions. The result is a nicely balanced group of seemingly real people who draw us into the play and make its teachings a part of us—which, after all, is Iriarte's purpose. This delicate balancing is actually best seen in the one-act *The Bookstore* where Feliciana represents the wholesome, sensible, perfect woman—the same creation although much less sketchily seen in Rosalía in *Winning Ways*. To oppose her the three exaggerated figures of Don Silvestre, Don Roque, and Don Isidro are introduced. In this particular play, really a *sainete*, the contrast is subdued by the music, the general levity, and the writer's gentle sarcasm smiling behind his creations. In all of Iriarte's plays (except his very first) there is little of the coldness, the woodenness, and the resulting blandness of most of his fellow Neoclassicists. The secret of his success was his sense of balance. And the secret of this equilibrium was Iriarte's comprehension of the truth behind the *utile dulci* concept: gentleness.

IV Guzmán el bueno (Guzmán, The Good)

From the plays presented here it can be seen that Iriarte cultivated various divisions of the dramatic art. In addition he introduced a genre into Spain that had a tremendous following in the late eighteenth century. The genre is the *melólogo* (melologue). The history of the melologue would be largely unknown if it were not for the excellent study by Subirá called *El compositor Iriarte (The Composer Iriarte)*. The interesting background of the field and the neglected importance of Iriarte in it have been made plain by Subirá. Iriarte wrote the first nationally popular melologue in Spanish: *Guzmán el bueno, Soliloquio ú escena trágica unipersonal, con música en sus intervalos (Guzmán, The Good, Soliloquy or Tragic Scene for One Person, with Music in its Intervals)*. This work was printed in 1790 and appeared on the stage only a few months before Iriarte's death in 1791. Its success was immediate. The play has no real plot but is essentially what its title indicates: a monologue by that venerated figure of Spanish history and literature, Alonso Pérez de Guzmán. Guzmán was the governor of Tarifa who, during the wars between Sancho IV (1284–1295) and this king's brother Juan, promised Sancho that he would not surrender the place. Juan led a Moslem army against Tarifa and threatened to kill Guzmán's infant son, whom he had captured, unless the city was handed over. Guzmán remained faithful to his king and even sent his own dagger for Juan to use to carry out his threat. Juan did have the boy beheaded in front of the walls of Tarifa, but was never able to take the town. The subject is a very popular one in Spanish literature.

Iriarte's short drama presents the emotional crisis of the father in the moments before the death of his son. The father goes through the gamut of all emotions possible as he wrestles with his conscience. The scene is very credible, and the dilemma of the father is portrayed in a quite realistic, acceptable fashion. The injection of music between the scenes, and particularly during the father's final monologue, heightens the effect upon the audience to a considerable degree. The resultant evocation of emotion is extraordinary and the reaction of the audience must have been one of stunned participation, thus creating a more immediate and lasting reaction than other treatments of this same theme in longer plays. The author's instructions for this final scene show exactly what was to be presented on the stage and indirectly what was to be awakened in the audience: "[Guzmán] again goes to the top of the wall while the orchestra plays a *Largo* very sadly with muted flutes. From there with the most expressive indications of pain he observes what is happening below; he comes down looking aghast, covering his face with both hands; he is to fall on the bench overwhelmed with grief; and with a hesitant voice full of anguish, the music accompanying all the while, he says: '. . . Oh, God! What have I seen? My son! You, lowering your head? You, your arms roughly bound. . . .'" [11]

It was Iriarte who popularized this type of play in Spain, introducing it from France where it had begun with Rousseau's *Pygmalion*. The melologue did not last long as a literary form but it did produce some well-known works like *L'Arlesienne* of Georges Bizet, originally with the words of Alphonse Daudet. Subirá tells us succinctly what the form was by quoting from the *Biographie Universelle Des Musiciens (Universal Biography of Musicians)*: " 'Melologue (from the Greek *melos*, music, and *logos*, discourse). Dramatic genre invented by Rousseau in which the orchestra carries on a dialogue with the words of the actor, who is on the stage to express with the help of the music the emotions that move him [in the particular situation].'" [12] Iriarte's importance rests in his popularization of the genre in Spain, although admittedly its popularity was somewhat ephemeral. Iriarte's play also brings out another facet of his writing—that of the musical composer. Subirá writes of this aspect of Iriarte's work in the most glowing terms: ". . . no one considers that he was also a musical composer . . . a truly distinguished one, whose prominence as an innovator can be perhaps compared to that of a Falla [with no exaggeration whatever]. . . ." [13] With this play—or melologue—Iriarte takes on a new dimension. He is more than an erudite writer about music as we saw in *Music;* he is more, too, than an admirer of contemporary composers; he is more than an able musician. He is a composer in his own right and as a result is responsible for creating an entirely new dramatic and musical vogue in Spain.

At the end of the chapter we realize that Iriarte is more versatile than any one critic has cared to assert. His production within the field of drama alone is enough to accord him recognition that has too long been denied him. In many ways he is the true father of the Neoclassic movement in Spanish drama. Such a claim is not at all as rash as it might initially appear, one hastens to add. The claim can be based on the points made in this chapter. First, Iriarte is in the vanguard of those who advocate reform of the theater—and who realistically seek to carry out their ideas of reform. He translated a large number of works in his first attempt to acclimate the Neoclassic precepts within the Spanish theater. Second, while writing his translations he created an original play, *The Busybody*, that, although unsuccessful through no great fault of his own, appeared in the same year, 1770, usually considered by critics as the one in which the Neoclassicists began to make their first thrust forward. It was noted too that Iriarte's defeat was hardly more ignominious than Moratín's even though the latter's play *Hormesinda* did reach the stage. Third, Iriarte wrote an essay that expounded many of the Neoclassic principles concerning drama, and at the same time sought to urge the Neoclassicists on in their labors. Fourth, Iriarte is the first Neoclassicist to produce a successful comedy. This achievement was noted even by his contemporaries, but later criticism has failed to applaud sufficiently this feat and its importance. In addition, Iriarte wrote a second comedy that was destined to be equally as good as the first, notwithstanding the poor performance of the actors. The last composition considered above, *Guzmán, The Good*, proves above all Iriarte's versatility. Not only does the play nationalize an entirely new genre; it places Iriarte within the field of musical creation, a field in which few other Spanish writers of the time could justly claim membership. It would appear therefore that a more open-minded attitude toward Iriarte's participation in Spanish drama is needed. For far too long his contributions have been, if not totally neglected, at least consciously disregarded.

CHAPTER 5

Iriarte and the Critics

I Origins of an Attitude Toward Iriarte

IN the preceding chapters of this book we have had both a general and a specific presentation of Iriarte's life and work. In the first chapter there was some mention of the writer's works as they affected his total development, and in the following three chapters there was a more detailed study of those works that either indicated important aspects of his literary maturation or were themselves the visible reasons for his popularity and renown. When considering the writer and his achievements from these standpoints, we never really delved into the matter of criticism except very briefly in the first chapter while noting the Iriarte-Forner polemic that affected and still affects the position of the fabulist in Spanish letters. The purpose of this final chapter therefore is to give a chronological view of the criticism that has been made of Iriarte. Especially among Iriarte's contemporaries, this criticism tended to be more negative and personal than was necessary. When not of outright disapproval, the tone was often one of benevolent indifference, and this tone has continued down to our own time. Much of this attitude can be attributed to that feeling of benign tolerance toward the Spanish eighteenth century held by entirely too many critics even today. There are very few commentators whose criticism has sought to understand what that century really was all about. Clichés and flippancy have characterized the principal attitudes. Much of the tone had its origin in the century itself from its more acerbic writers. Much of it is due also to the reaction by the Romantic movement against a thesis it found unpalatable. But much of the blame still falls on critics from the nineteenth century on who have refused to be impartial in their judgments of the eighteenth century, either because they are too fond of the Golden Age to see its faults or because they are too fond of the Romantic spirit and its legacy. The feeling of benevolence, tolerance, or whatever one may wish to call it, is seen very early in the criticism of Iriarte's work. The attitude has been a natural result of the way in which the criticism began. To study the history of Iriartean criticism we must return to the bittter conflict between Iriarte and Forner.

It will be remembered that before 1780 Iriarte had become involved in public disagreements with several people and that he had written certain essays supporting his views. Such was the case in the Sedano affair in the late 1770's. Iriarte wrote another work that appeared in 1781. It was a defense of his eclogue, *La felicidad de la vida del campo (The Happiness of Country Life)*, submitted to the Royal Academy competition for 1779. In that competition Iriarte's poem had been awarded second place to Meléndez Valdés' eclogue, *Batilo*. Most critics have seen in Iriarte's polemical *Reflexiones sobre la égloga de Batilo (Reflections on the Eclogue Batilo)* only a vicious attack on Meléndez Valdés, a virtual unknown at that time. They have tended to overlook the valid criticism made and have considered it only the result of a young, wounded vanity. Even a critic as fair as Fernando Lázaro, the editor of Forner noted earlier, in our day at times uses a completely unacceptable and biased tone toward Iriarte.[1] Juan Pablo Forner wrote in 1781 in reply to Tomás de Iriarte's essay a pamphlet entitled *Cotejo de las églogas que ha premiado la Real Academia de la Lengua (Comparison of the Eclogues Awarded Prizes by the Royal Academy of the Language)*. He saw a means of enhancing his own stature, which was admittedly quite small at this stage, by continuing and expanding the debate that had so conveniently arisen. Although his work is essentially a defense of Meléndez Valdés and, even more important, a treatise on the purpose and form of poetry, it is from a realistic viewpoint principally a means of attacking an established writer to further Forner's own ends. He felt that his reputation could easily be strengthened by attacking so popular a figure as Iriarte. As a recent article points out, from this date on Iriarte was to be an obsession with Forner, so much so that he would continue to condemn and recondemn him for the next ten years.[2] *The Erudite Ass* was to follow immediately the publication of the *Literary Fables* in 1782. Iriarte in reply then wrote *For Just Such Cases* to which Forner responded with *Los gramáticos: historia chinesca (The Grammarians: A Chinese History)*. There were further unpleasantries exchanged, but this is enough to re-

mind us of the situation existing for Iriarte in the 1780's when his fame was greatest. The beginning of the negative attitude toward him thus has its origin in a vicious critic who more than anything else was always seeking to further his own aims.

What Forner says in the *Comparison* is essentially what he was to repeat ad nauseam. One does not mean to infer that some of his ideas are not valid. Much of what he says is pertinent but it loses its force in part because of the personal hatred it reveals for Iriarte. The position Forner takes while considering Iriarte's work is totally negative; in addition, it is mocking and belittling. Since it is against a man who was well known, it is to be expected that Forner's diatribes might delight that segment of the literati more given to personal vituperation. Iriarte's style of writing—the "prosaic" or unpoetic quality of his verse—was the main preoccupation of Forner and it has continued to concern critics down to our own day. At the end of his essay Forner bluntly states his feelings concerning Iriarte's poem—and Iriarte himself. There is nothing redeeming in the poetry, he would imply, from the standpoint of character development, atmosphere, or message, and certainly there is nothing worthwhile in the style: "I conclude then by saying that in the work of Mr. Cisneros [Iriarte] besides there being no color or bucolic style, there is no color or universal style; that his expression is exaggerated in part, base in another, languid here, and violent there; that his personages express themselves at times like poets, others like very urbane people, others like philosophers, others like politicians and others like hermits . . . their language . . . is of an elegance foreign to our poetry in which it is not always correct to introduce sentences of a *prosaic style* [italics mine] . . . but . . . the author will attribute all that is said here to calumny and the desire to malign. . . ."[3]

There are two points in this commentary that should be emphasized. The one statement, noted above, has been placed in italics. The other idea becomes just as current: that Iriarte could not accept criticism and rather than follow the critics' advice he preferred to ignore it, attributing their statements to personal jealousy or rancor. There is no doubt that Iriarte disliked criticism, especially the vituperative kind to which he was subjected. But we have seen the moderation with which he ordinarily replied to his detractors. Indeed he exhibits little of the shrill pettiness one finds in Forner. And we must remember that this restraint

comes from a person who was always youthful, volatile, even impetuous. The idea that Iriarte discounted criticism of his work because he thought the critics jealous must have certain qualifications. First, unfortunately for himself and contradictory to what Forner writes, he did not ignore it and got involved in the polemics as a result. Second, Forner and others were right in one respect—Iriarte did understand that so much of the outcry was due solely to envy. Had Forner, for example, not been so inordinately jealous, he would never have written this particular essay. The fact that there is some valid literary criticism in the work does not deny this less acceptable reason for writing in the first place. It might be added too that had Forner's envy not been so great, Iriarte could perhaps have lived, if not longer, more healthfully. As it was, he felt obliged to reply to the needless attacks, and in his works he time and again states his weariness brought on by the mental and emotional strain.

As the Fornerian type of criticism began to circulate, the popularity of Iriarte still continued to grow. The duality of commentary by two factions, one disgruntled and envious and the other equally blind in its praise, must be understood in order to appreciate the difficult position of Iriarte. Another selection from Pignatelli's essay written only a few years after Forner's words above is appropriate:

Finally, my friend [Bernardo de Iriarte], I have only to say to you that you have given to the emulators of your brother who . . . still sprout up a new bone to gnaw with this new edition [1805]. They have no consolation whatever in seeing that the works of Iriarte are sought and appreciated, that all his productions are quickly bought up, that his *Fables* are known by heart, just like others of his poems, and that his name is already classic in Spanish literature. [Another short quotation fits in very well here also because it is a retort, although a veiled one, to Forner's attitude. Speaking of Iriarte's aims and desires regarding style, Pignatelli writes:] . . . he could not stand the Gallomania that reigned in his time in some Spaniards. . . . But at the same time he could not countenance the tenacious and ill-founded pride with which some of his countrymen either believed or affected to believe that we know everything. . . . In whatever work that might be presented to him, the first thing that called his attention was its soundness, the unity of its thought, and the all-important objective of instruction. . . . *Therefore he so much abhorred poetry*

[132]

that consists only of pompous words, and harmony with no real substance was nothing for him [italics mine].[4]

This is an indirect defense of Iriarte's style and tone but one that was to become lost in the total development of the criticism of him. Very few indeed would be those who defended Iriarte's "poetic prosaism."

With the establishment of the Fornerian brand of criticism, variations in it soon began to appear. It is quite easy for Larra some thirty to forty years later to set Iriarte apart, innocently enough to be sure, but still to make him part of an attitude in which a truly lyric tone supposedly is lacking. He writes:

Ayala, Luzán, Huerta, Moratín senior, Meléndez Valdés, Jovellanos, Cienfuegos, and some others, restored *belles lettres* it is true, but how? By introducing into our eighteenth century the French taste just as in the sixteenth others had introduced the Italian. They were imitators, without knowing it most of the time, objecting to such an idea almost always. The spirit of analysis, of dissection, let us say, and the French philosophical spirit made their influence felt in our literary regeneration. The agents [of this regeneration] wanting above all to be thought independent tried to save the *expression* of our former failure; that is, on adopting the French ideas of the eighteenth century they sought to express them with our language of the sixteenth century. Once pure, they considered themselves original. Thus once we saw preserved in poetry the poetic knowledge of our good times we seemed to hear still the work of Herrera and Rioja; and in prose any innovation in the language of Cervantes was declared a crime. Iriarte, Cadalso, and others declared themselves purists at all times, and pursued any new mode of expression with the arms of satire while Meléndez, Jovellanos, Huerta, and Moratín maintained the same opinion through example.[5]

Even though one may question Larra's basic assertion since we have seen in the case of Iriarte alone that neither is he so rigid nor is his basic aim so narrow, the quotation is in intriguing contrast to Pignatelli's. In general it is a typically Romantic attitude toward the eighteenth century. Here and elsewhere Larra is really more interested in what Iriarte had to say and not how he said it. He considers Iriarte's mode of expression as evidenced in *Music* or in the *Literary Fables* less important than what he had to say in these and others of his more satirical productions.

The emphasis is placed on the critical and not the creative aspect of Iriarte's work.

From Larra's statement it is only a short step to one by Quintana in which we find succinctly declared the view of Iriarte's talents held in the early and mid-nineteenth century. It is a view that will be amplified, too much perhaps, in the ensuing years. Quintana's picture is too cold, too precise really to portray Iriarte and his work adequately. His tone and his intention dismiss the writer too quickly. We have seen on various occasions that Iriarte is too complex a man and too profound a poet to be reviewed easily. Quintana prefers to see nothing under Iriarte's smooth, polished exterior. After him other critics have done the very same thing. Moreover, what Quintana has to say about some of Iriarte's works is questionable. To say that Iriarte was not a poet in this poem but that he was in another, and so on, is to be too autocratic and, worse, to forget the basic reasons for Iriarte's writing certain works at certain times. The matter of prosaic poetry, although not too blatantly, is apparent throughout. Quintana writes in a short article entitled "Iriarte—Samaniego—Prosaísmo":

All that well-formed reason, selective erudition, and a natural discretion cultivated with the most urbane treatment from the court could procure in regard to regularity, judgment, polish, and elegance for a lively and bright talent, as much and more this writer put into his works which soon notably excited the public's attention and gave him great renown. But if these qualities were enough in the average and more temperate genres, they were not in those which require much elevation of spirit, great flights into fantasy, vivacity in the expression of emotion, charm and strength in color, and number and flexibility in sound. In these endowments, which are the truly great poetic media, Iriarte was entirely lacking. Thus, while a poet frequently in his fables and sometimes in his epistles, epigrams, and light verse, he is never one in the poem *Music,* which is more a treatise than a poem.[6]

II *Establishment of the Attitude*

For Quintana's tone to continue, all that was needed was someone with more prestige as a critic to make use of it. This person was Menéndez y Pelayo. With his pronouncements the characterization of Iriarte's style became fixed. Most investigators from that time on have merely followed what he said. One does not mean to imply that there was necessarily a conscious imitation

of Menéndez. It is just that his attitude, so wholly of the nineteenth century, was the most heard and therefore the most influential. Again, it is an attitude toward the entire eighteenth
century and not just toward one specific author in it. The tone
employed by Menéndez is one of near condescension. There is a
recognition of what the eighteenth-century writers did or attempted to do, but it is always an acknowledgment of their
colder, more precise vein. Much attention is paid to their criticism
and their satire. The polemical involvements of so many of the
previous century's authors attract Menéndez and his disciples because the quarrels only emphasize those authors' so-called prosaic
side. Although there is some attempt to understand a lyrical strain
running beneath the surface, it is actually very half-hearted. It is
as if the nineteenth-century critics wished to deny any possibility
of lyrical creativity in their immediate predecessors. When writing
of Iriarte in his *Horacio en España (Horace in Spain)*, Menéndez
y Pelayo does acknowledge some of Iriarte's merit, but he indirectly dismisses so much of the poet's total work that the
modern-day reader is disappointed by his statements. In the
following selection Menéndez compares Iriarte to his mentor
Horace. In the comparison Iriarte takes second place, a fact that
one cannot dispute. It is, however, in the assertions about Iriarte's
inherent coldness and lack of poetic fantasy that one becomes
skeptical. Too much emphasis is placed on Iriarte's failure to
open up, to permit himself to feel and express his emotion. Such
a contention is to miss the underlying feeling of the Neoclassic
writers entirely. If not this, it is certainly a failure to accept them
for what they were without the prejudices of a later, different
mentality. Menéndez has the following to say about Iriarte:

   To the literary group *La Tertulia de la Fonda de San Sebastián*
belonged, as did Cadalso and Moratín senior, Tomás de Iriarte; although this literary scholar lacked lyrical genius, he formed a school
apart with entirely too many disciples as an instigator of prosaism.
But here he does merit praise for the eleven ingenious epistles concerning literary matters inserted in the second volume of his works.
It would be ridiculous to ask in essays of that type for great poetic
spirit or a notable wealth of style. . . . The epistles of Iriarte are
sermons, in imitation of Horace. . . . The Horatian sentence is always
poetic and pure, and the hexameters [of certain poems] . . . can
hardly be confused with prose, although neither do they resemble the

[135]

TOMÁS DE IRIARTE

hexameters of the *Aeneid*. But apart from this defect, which in Iriarte
comes from his taste and transcended all his works, apart from the
natural coldness of the writer which never permits him to be moved
or to become very angry, those epistles, especially the first four and
the seventh, are his best titles of literary nobility after the *Fables* and
the play *The Pampered Youth*.[7]

A selection from the *Historia de las ideas estéticas en España*
(*History of Aesthetic Ideas in Spain*) elaborates on the above
theme although it does little to improve Menéndez' idea of
Iriarte as a poet. In Volume III we find:

Iriarte possessed all the good literary qualities except those that are
born from the zeal of fantasy. All his erudition and good taste were
not enough to make him understand or feel the difference between
poetry and prose; but this latter, as well as being his first, is his only
defect. In everything else he is correct and discreet. If one reads his
works like critical prose, there will be nothing to fault in them. His
work does not possess sentiment, images, or anything that we com-
monly call poetry; but it does possess freedom of style, a cultural
grace, good taste, all the qualities that can make one read a book with
pleasure but never to become enthusiastic about it. . . . Iriarte was
considered an admirer and disciple of Horace, the man who had the
greatest poetic style in the world, and he translated [Horace] faith-
fully as well as colorlessly, and he read him incessantly and counted
him among his intimate friends.[8]

At the end of the nineteenth century Iriarte's greatest biog-
rapher and expositor, Cotarelo, writes much in the same words
of Menéndez. Cotarelo, however, does try to seek some explanation for the tone and ambience of the poet's work. When he discusses the content of Iriarte's various compositions, usually at
some length, he almost always puzzles over their prosaic quality
and resulting lack of verve. Iriarte's translation of the *Poetics*
does not escape this inquiry. In fact, Cotarelo ends up sounding
very much like Menéndez when he notes the "capital defects" of
Iriarte's effort. It is almost as if he and Menéndez y Pelayo want
to see a duplicate of the original, which would be impossible anyway. They are not willing to accept the intrusion of the translator's
style and outlook, both of which are bound to become evident
no matter who the translator might be: "The capital defects of
this work are those common to other works of the illustrious

[136]

Canarian; that is, the lack of number, intonation, and poetic verve . . . and the diffuse, diluted quality of the instruction; since although the author tries to conjure away this charge citing the different structure of the languages regarding conciseness and citing examples . . . he will always be very redundant, just as his contemporaries told him." [9]

Cotarelo's effort to explain Iriarte's style is laudable, and it does indicate some sort of attempt, however weak and ineffective, to understand the poet—something few critics had done before. The following long quotation is included to show to what lengths Cotarelo does go in treating this matter. His statements are valid even if they do not represent a total comprehension:

To what must we attribute, therefore, the prosaism, the lack of vitality, of number, and elevation that is noted in his verse? How could an alert imagination . . . a sharp and fertile genius, a very clear intelligence, and a memory nurtured on the best models give such results? Two facts alone can give the explanation of the phenomenon. First and foremost was education. Tomás de Iriarte is the realization of the ideal conceived by his uncle Juan de Iriarte . . . a man for whom poetry was no more than the art of expressing all that is ordinarily written in prose but in an ingenious, clear way and with the help of rhyme. He conceded no substance whatever to poetry and relegated it to a secondary position of service, at times in order to reduce determined precepts to formulas, at times to make the wit of a clever phrase stand out more, or at times to express in a less common way but always with mathematical precision ideas suggested to him by events of more than ordinary importance. If by chance some spark of imagination appeared, he preserved it for his verses in Latin which he constructed with classic elegance. For this reason he wrote his Latin Grammar in verse so that its rules could be easily memorized, and for this same reason he made and unmade epigrams . . . in order to present them in the briefest, clearest, and most brilliant form possible. . . . He [Tomás de Iriarte] later fell under the direction of that icy, prosaic, and utilitarian spirit of his older brother whom he did not really know until he came to Madrid, who was almost twice his age, whom he considered a father, with whom he used the formal *usted*, and who exercised a kind of intellectual tutelage over his two younger brothers. . . . Vanity, so characteristic of this family and especially of Don Tomás, caused him at all times to avoid anything that might present a pretext for the ridiculous and even for the temperate censure of his emulators. He was always very sensitive to criticism, and thus when his imagination tried to reveal itself in his works

TOMÁS DE IRIARTE

with any spirit, a severe, continuous, inexplorable polishing . . . put
out those flames and the writer surprised himself at his own daring.
The second reason or cause of Iriarte's prosaism is more a generic one
and a common one of the period: prosaism, as an illustrious writer has
said, was in the atmosphere of the eighteenth century; it had been
born in the previous century as a natural reaction to euphuism, arising
from the ruin of a poetic ideal not yet replaced by another. Iriarte
only accommodated himself to his time, therefore; he did not bring or
invent prosaism; rather he ennobled and adorned it with decency,
and this was his great sin only because of bad example. If he had had
another literary education, he would have protested against that tendency and would have been a great poet in the modern sense of the
word.[10]

The problem with Iriarte as Cotarelo saw it was much that of
the majority of eighteenth-century writers. He was too bound by
restraint or at least by an exaggerated sense of moderation. The
inability to transcend these boundaries was the major shortcom-
ing of Iriarte according to Cotarelo's thesis. Again it must be
emphasized that Cotarelo is not condemning the fabulist so
roundly as Menéndez y Pelayo did, for Cotarelo honestly seeks to
find a reasonable reply to the criticism that has its origin and
propagation in Forner. The real solution is not to explain the
situation through reasons of heritage or background, however.
Rather, another approach must be made toward comprehending
the attitude expressed in Iriarte's poetry: Iriarte must have meant
to write as he did, so why not try to understand the conscious
reason for his doing so. The matter then becomes one of aesthetics
and leaves the realm of psychology where Cotarelo, quite early it
might be noted, so diligently tried to put it. At the end of the
nineteenth century we can say that the criticism of Iriarte has
still not tried to understand fully his literary criteria and is following the old assertions of Forner, later more clearly formulated
and formalized by Menéndez y Pelayo.

III Advancement of a New Idea

The attempt to reorient the thinking about Iriarte's style does
not occur until quite recently. Among the first who try to be a
bit more imaginative in their criticism, whether productive or
not, is Alberto Navarro González, who wrote an article entitled
"Temas humanos en la poesía de Iriarte" ("Human Themes in the

Poetry of Iriarte") that appeared in *Revista de literatura* in 1952. At the beginning he divides Iriarte's poetry into two groups, one composed of those poems with a frivolous intent and the other, those of a more serious nature. Navarro makes an initial statement that is no different from earlier commentary: " . . . critics have quite rightly spoken of prosaism [in Iriarte's work] and have limited themselves to praising the facile, harmonious versification and elegant, pure language. . . . Certainly, for an aesthetic that values primarily the participation of sentiment in the literary work, neither Iriarte nor his epoch would hold an outstanding position. On one hand, distrusting any construction that tries to stand without the support of the senses or of reason, they consider poetry more as a receptacle for beneficial or entertaining ideas than for deep sentiments; and on the other, enthusiasm is reserved especially for themes of immediate social interest, with the rare appearance of eternal, individual preoccupations." [11]

When writing of Iriarte's disapproval of life in the capital, a theme Navarro finds intriguing, he goes beyond the trite statements just quoted to write: "Iriarte does not intimately despise the life of the court. To the contrary, it constitutes his real life, and it is precisely his fondness for it that draws out his complaints against the imperfections that deform it. The theme is a traditional one and can be seen in La Bruyère; Iriarte, however, writes with a heat and truth not too common in his century and, if for reasons different from those of Villarroel, Meléndez Valdés, and Cadalso, the old theme of the contempt for city life quite authentically reappears." [12] After discussing another theme, that of the troubles poetic composition brings its creator, Navarro adds: "Reading other compositions in which he speaks even more passionately, we see how the Canarian writer reaches the conclusion that it is well to write poetry but not to publish it, to create but not to expose one's work to the judgment of evil-minded enemies." [13] This is a theme we have seen in Iriarte's poetry, and it is interesting to find it used here in order to denote a more melancholy, disillusioned Iriarte than had been heretofore admitted. Concluding his short essay, Navarro has the following points:

> Iriarte, discovering the incapacity of poetry to give him the present he would like and the assurance of a real future, disregarding any other altruistic or transcendental end, not only limits himself in rela-

tion to the distraction it provides him but he also runs the danger of becoming inactive or bestial. . . . The public does not wish to be edified or taught; Iriarte does not have new and beautiful things to give it [Iriarte thinks]; therefore, desperate, the only thing he feels he can do is to brandish his swords in empty air for his own diversion, ending up consequently in a sort of inactivity and bestiality [one is appalled at Navarro's insistent attitude and choice of words here] . . . even if [the poems under consideration] cannot be placed precisely beside the beautiful compositions that form the white fire from the depths of the souls of Jorge Manrique, Garcilaso, Fray Luis de León, San Juan de la Cruz, Bécquer, or Antonio Machado, they should nevertheless not ever be missing in an anthology that brings together the best poetry of our eighteenth century.[14]

This stage of the development of Iriartean criticism is significant because in it there is obviously some slight attempt, although hardly a feeling or successful one, to accept Iriarte as an artist, an innovator with truly creative abilities. This is a far cry from the acceptance of him as a rhetorician, or, worse, an idle purveyor of rules. From the title of the article on, the author seeks to prove the merits of the eighteenth-century fabulist that have been overlooked or denied. The fact that Navarro even considers themes in the poetry is indicative of his attitude especially when the majority of previous critics had ceaselessly reviewed the style, the rules, the coldness, the recipients of the attacks, etc. That an effort is made to approach the subject more objectively, more open-mindedly is what interests us here. It should not be inferred that all the information is important or even interesting. A great deal of it is trite and of little real value in understanding the poet because Navarro does not elaborate his themes enough. There is a tendency to accumulate the examples but to not tie them together very well. In fact, much of what he says is nothing more than what had been written before, only treated this time in a different way and with a different purpose in mind. And here naturally is the reason for his criticism's importance.

We come then to the final stage that Iriartean criticism takes. The next essay concerning Iriarte's style and intentions is published some ten years later in 1960. It goes much beyond Navarro's efforts and in general may be considered an amplification, in a negative sort of way, of what the latter wrote in the early 1950's. The reaction against some of Navarro's truisms thus gives us the first and, to this date, the only real attempt to understand Iriarte's aesthetic principles. With this publication we must say that at last, nearly two hundred years after Iriarte's death, criticism of the poet has reached its long-awaited maturity and impartiality. Near the beginning of his short book on Iriarte, *Tomás de Iriarte: Poeta de "rapto racional"* (*Tomás de Iriarte: Poet of "Rational Ecstasy"*) Russell Sebold writes of the history of the attitude toward the poet and of what his own attitude will be: "Attention has also been called to the more or less anecdotal and external aspects of the *Fables*, like their costumbrism, their humor, their didactic value, the principal sources of the literary precepts dramatized in them, the possible allusions contained in them to contemporary writers, the personal motives of Iriarte to write in the old genre of Aesop, and the fundamental Iriartean rules for the apologue. But there has never been any attempt to point out, on the basis of the internal esthetic principles of Iriarte's work, how he proceeds to create poetry . . . that is to say, precisely what makes him, in addition to a versifier, a poet." [15]

Sebold's intention is to explore and to emphasize that side of Iriarte which has been quite thoroughly neglected. To do this he discusses the Neoclassic and Romantic mentalities, presenting some ideas that are particularly applicable to Iriarte and to what the critics have said about him: "To sum up, Neoclassic poetry differs from the Romantic not because one lacks the stamp of the poet and the other does not, but because in Neoclassic poetry one notes the presence of the poet only *a posteriori* while in the Romantic one notes it *a priori*. In each one *Nature* and the medium are of equal importance; but one reaches the personality of the Neoclassicist by first understanding the particular internal harmony of his work, while the personality of the poet is the only possible point of departure in order to understand a Romantic poem like, for example, the *Song to Teresa* [by Espronceda]." [16] Leading us up to a comprehension of his own vision of Iriarte, Sebold writes: ". . . Hugh Blair observed that the word *beauty* is applied 'to various dispositions of the mind; and even more, to various objects of abstract science. We speak frequently of a beautiful tree or flower, of a beautiful poem, of a beautiful character, and of *a beautiful mathematical theorem*'. . . . A few years after the death of [Samuel] Johnson, Iriarte, and Blair, Quintana would compose his celebrated ode *To the Spanish Expedition to*

Propagate Vaccine in America. Science was poetry, and poetry was science. . . ." [17] At this point we understand that it is exactly this attitude of "rational ecstasy" that Sebold finds in Iriarte and that also serves as the basis for his appraisal of the poet. He concludes his general views with some statements that nicely negate all those criticisms of the prosaism of the Neoclassicists: "Finally, perhaps all poetry should approach, in the greatest possible degree, the prose of its period . . . not only as a safeguard against affectation but as a guarantee that what is essential and spontaneous in the human context of its historical period be captured. (What was human in the period of full rationalism was to not emphasize what was human.)" [18]

Sebold's idea is that, for Iriarte, poetry was a creation of simplicity and nobility, those same characteristics to be always demanded of good prose. Referring to a sonnet of Iriarte in which he finds this concept neatly expressed or, rather, implied, he writes: "There is in this sonnet a prelude to the delicateness and melody of the *Rhymes* of Bécquer (who, it will be remembered, studied with the Neoclassicist Lista), to the sunny and bittersweet tranquility of the gardens of Juan Ramón Jiménez, and to the images of García Lorca . . . besides the echoes of the poetry of Garcilaso. But it will be noted that in the entire sonnet there is no image or construction that would not be natural in a noble and simple prose." [19] Sebold concludes his study with the following very opportune words: "Above all, there has to be a re-evaluation, from within the artistic context of the Neoclassic works, of the role of the eighteenth-century reform and didactic preoccupations. In some cases—especially Iriarte's apologues—*utility,* or better the *appearance of utility,* is nothing but a springboard in order to arrive at an esthetic value." [20]

This is the attitude that has so long been needed in order to appreciate eighteenth-century ideas and ideals. Sebold is the first modern critic who tries with a sense of fairness and objectivity to accept Iriarte on his own terms and not to consider him from moral or aesthetic principles of a later day. The attitude indicates that at last a judgment can be made about the Neoclassic Spanish writers without its being either totally laudatory or condemning. Such a perspective is indeed refreshing and, one might add, past due. For our own purposes, the criticism is naturally all the more pertinent because with it we see that Iriarte is no longer the cold, unfeeling author who possesses no really creative vision. It should be noted that Sebold does not include *Music* or the poem *The Happiness of Country Life* in his new approach to Iriarte's aesthetics. He would, we assume, consider them too lacking in the *dulci* aspect of the Horatian maxim. For his taste, and that of all previous critics, *Music* too obviously instructs with little stylistic grace to save it from pedantry and tedium. Whether the reader wishes to agree or not with this view is beside the point. The true significance of this essay is its honest reappraisal of Iriarte and his work.

IV *Conclusion*

Throughout this book we have dealt with Iriarte from various standpoints: his life and personality in general, his work in general and in particular, and the attitudes that have surrounded him from his own day down to the middle of the twentieth century. Each chapter, especially those that treated his works more specifically, had some definite theme uniting the directions of discussion in them. The second chapter showed how by the time Iriarte had reached his physical maturity he had also reached a certain maturation point in his literary production. The translation of the *Poetics*, the essay in its defense, and the resulting poem *Music* all indicate a degree of thought and a completion of his ideas concerning style that engendered the physical work of the *Literary Fables*. This particular work itself, as seen in Chapter Three, represents the apogee of Iriarte's attitudes and indeed his artistic genius. The collection stands as a monument to his best ideas about literary creation and, even more important, it is in itself an ingenious literary creation. It teaches and entertains, embodying both parts of the Horatian precept. This feat, so well proved by the book's continuous popularity, shows better than any other single work the ingenuity, the inherent creativeness, and the resultant success that Neoclassicism did have in Spain. But it is not only in the genre of the fable that Iriarte has merited renown. Chapter Four pointed out the veritable wealth that Iriarte left in the dramatic genre—a legacy that is only recently being appreciated. And in this final chapter we have seen how criticism of Iriarte, the artist, is beginning to change its viewpoint also.

To conclude, we must make several affirmative statements. To the question of exactly what Iriarte has left us, we can answer easily with a gesture toward his wide, varied production that is even yet in great part inadequately appreciated. We can point out his happy pronouncement of the *utile dulci* theme and his effective use of it in all his works, a feat not often achieved in Spain in the eighteenth century. The realization of his idea is not only visible in the *Literary Fables* but in less-known works like the drama *The Pampered Youth* or the melologue *Guzmán, The Good*. These statements naturally lead us to the following—that he is the most adequate representative of Neoclassicism in Spain. They further cause us to affirm that Iriarte is the best representative of what the Spanish eighteenth century had the potential for being—forever seeking, but with positive goals; fruitful, but not overripe or exaggeratedly exuberant. And in exhibiting these particular traits Iriarte continues, ironically perhaps, given the negative criticism that has generally plagued him, that sober yet paradoxically effusive vein in Spanish literature seen throughout the centuries—he is simply its eighteenth-century manifestation.

Notes and References

Chapter One

1. José de Viera y Clavijo, *Noticias de la historia general de las Islas Canarias*, III (Santa Cruz de Tenerife: Goya-Ediciones, 1952— first published in 1783), 472.

2. Emilio Cotarelo y Mori, *Iriarte y su época* (Madrid: Est. Tipográfico "Sucesores de Rivadeneyra," 1897), p. 30. For further information on Juan de Iriarte see pp. 1–30 of Cotarelo.

3. *Ibid.*, p. 431. Cotarelo provides the baptismal certificate from the archives of the church.

4. Martín Fernández Navarrete, "Noticias biográficas y juicios críticos," *Poetas líricos del siglo XVIII*, II in *BAE* 63 (Madrid: Librería y Casa Editorial Hernando, 1925), 1.

5. Cotarelo, p. 51.

6. *Ibid.*, pp. 65–68.

7. *Ibid.*, pp. 434–35, quoting from *Papeles de Iriarte, sin signatura*, Biblioteca Nacional.

8. Cotarelo, "Cartas inéditas de Cadalso," *La España Moderna*, 73 (enero, 1895), 60–96. Raymond Foulché-Delbosc, "Obras inéditas de don José Cadalso," *Revue Hispanique*, I (1894), 258–328.

9. Cotarelo, *Iriarte y su época*, p. 149.

10. Antonio Aguirre, "La Notice De Carlos Pignatelli Sur Thomas De Yriarte," *Revue Hispanique*, 36 (1916), 249.

11. Tomás de Iriarte, *Colección de obras en verso y prosa*, II (Madrid: En la Imprenta de Benito Cano, 1787), 85–86. Whenever Iriarte's *Obras* are referred to hereafter, it is the 1787 edition unless otherwise specified.

12. It was this same syndrome which caused the first editor of *Don Quixote* to be relegated into obscurity. See my *The Rev. John Bowle: The Genesis of Cervantean Criticism* (Chapel Hill: The University of North Carolina Press, 1971).

13. Cotarelo, *Iriarte y su época*, p. 172.

14. *Ibid.*, pp. 184–89.

15. *Ibid.*, pp. 463 and 465, quoting from *Carta a D. Enrique Ramos* (1779), MS U–169 in the Biblioteca Nacional.

16. *Ibid.*, pp. 219–20, quoting from the *Gaceta* of March 28, 1780.

17. Juan Pablo Forner, *Cotejo de las églogas que ha premiado la Real Academia de la Lengua*, ed. Fernando Lázaro (Salamanca: Consejo Superior de Investigaciones Científicas, 1951), p. xix.
18. *Ibid.*, pp. xx–xxi, ed. quoting Forner MS 9584, pp. 304–8, in the Biblioteca Nacional.
19. Viera y Clavijo, p. 474.
20. Aguirre, p. 226.
21. Cotarelo, *Iriarte y su época*, p. 208, quoting Pellicer MS Jj–148, Biblioteca Nacional.
22. Aguirre, p. 231.
23. Cotarelo, *Iriarte y su época*, pp. 230–31, quoting from Bernardo de Iriarte, Archivo General Central de Alcalá, leg. 2.817.
24. *Ibid.*, p. 232, quoting from the *Reflexiones* (no page given).
25. *Ibid.*, p. 233.
26. *Ibid.*, p. 468, quoting from a letter to the Marqués de Manca on Aug. 1, 1781, in Papeles de Iriarte sin catalogar, Biblioteca Nacional.
27. *Ibid.*, pp. 470–71.
28. *Ibid.*, p. 475, quoting from a letter to the Marqués de Manca on Aug. 22, 1781, in Papeles de Iriarte sin catalogar, Biblioteca Nacional.
29. *Ibid.*, p. 244.
30. *Ibid.*, p. 251.
31. François Vézinet, *Molière, Florian Et La Littérature Espagnole* (Paris: Librairie Hachette Et. Cie., 1909), p. 233.
32. Cotarelo, *Iriarte y su época*, p. 252.
33. Aguirre, p. 233.
34. Forner, pp. xxi–xxii, ed. quoting Forner MS 9584, p. 309, in the Biblioteca Nacional.
35. Cotarelo, *Iriarte y su época*, p. 258.
36. Félix María de Samaniego, "Poesías," *Poetas líricos del siglo XVIII*, I in *BAE*, 61 (Madrid: Imprenta de los Sucesores de Hernando, 1921), 366.
37. Iriarte, *Obras*, I, 1.
38. *Ibid.*, VI, 370.
39. For more details see Félix María de Samaniego, *Obras inéditas o poco conocidas del insigne fabulista D. Félix María de Samaniego, precedidas de una biografía del autor escrita por D. Estaquio Fernández de Navarrete* (Vitoria: Imprenta de los Hijos de Manteli, 1866).
40. Forner, p. xx, ed. quoting Forner MS 9584, pp. 304–8, in the Biblioteca Nacional.
41. Cotarelo, *Iriarte y su época*, p. 275.
42. Iriarte, *Obras*, VI, 300, 315–17.

Notes and References

43. Marcelino Menéndez y Pelayo, *Historia de los heterodoxos españoles*, V, ed. Enrique Sánchez Reyes (Santander: Aldus, S.A. de Artes Gráficas, 1947), 306–7.

44. Masson de Morvilliers, "Espagne," *Encyclopédie Méthodique. Géographie*, I (Paris, 1783), 565.

45. Cotarelo, *Iriarte y su época*, pp. 315–16, quoting from Bernardo de Iriarte, Archivo General Central de Alcalá, leg. 2.817.

46. *Ibid.*, p. 323, quoting Tomás de Iriarte, Colección de varios papeles sueltos pertenecientes a Iriarte, Biblioteca Nacional.

47. It is interesting to note among the list of subscribers to this first edition of Iriarte's works the names of Benjamin Franklin and Thomas Jefferson, each of whom ordered two copies.

48. Juan Sempere y Guarinos, *Ensayo de una biblioteca española de los mejores escritores del reynado de Carlos III*, VI, quoting from the *censura* made by Santos Díez González (Madrid: Imprenta Real, 1785–1789), 211–12, 214.

49. Cotarelo, *Iriarte y su época*, p. 362, quoting from *La Espigadera*, t. II, 49 on.

50. Aguirre, pp. 240–41.

51. There is truly a dearth of material about Iriarte's relations with women. He did not marry. Other than in his letters where he sometimes makes references to women as he saw them at social functions or in some plays where a respect for them and a regret for their inferior social position are evidenced, one finds little in fact about this aspect of Iriarte's life. Cotarelo and Pignatelli do note his popularity with the fair sex but unfortunately Iriarte himself says virtually nothing.

52. Pignatelli, pp. 244–45.

53. *Ibid.*, p. 247.

Chapter Two

1. Iriarte, *Obras*, II, 84–86.

2. *Ibid.*, p. 100.

3. *Ibid.*, IV, xlii–xliv. Iriarte states that the editions of the poem he studied most carefully were the edition of 1629, the London edition of 1737, and the Glasgow edition of 1760. He studied others illustrated with notes and commentaries. He also explains how he proceeded with the editions: "Not guiding myself only by my own sense, but consulting the annotations of these learned men for obscure or doubtful places, I always adopted that reading and sense in which the majority of the commentators agree and which seem the most natural and probable."

4. *Ibid.*, p. iii.

5. *Ibid.*, pp. xix–xx.

6. *Ibid.*, p. xxii.

[147]

7. *Ibid.*, pp. xxi–xxii.

8. *Ibid.*, pp. xlvi–xlviii.

9. *Ibid.*, pp. li–lii.

10. *Ibid.*, pp. l–li.

11. *Ibid.*, pp. 22–23.

12. *Ibid.*, p. 44.

13. *Ibid.*, pp. 47–48. The Latin reads: *Omne tulit punctum, qui miscuit utile dulci.* . . .

14. *Ibid.*, pp. xliv–xlvi and pp. 9–10.

15. Cotarelo, *Iriarte y su época*, p. 160.

16. Iriarte, *Obras*, VI, ii–iii.

17. *Ibid.*, p. 10.

18. *Ibid.*, pp. 14–15.

19. *Ibid.*, p. 23.

20. *Ibid.*, pp. 45–47.

21. *Ibid.*, p. 85.

22. *Ibid.*, pp. 151, 186–95.

23. *Ibid.*, pp. 228–29.

24. See Chapter 1 of this book for more details on the polemic between Sedano and Ríos. See also pages 235 on of *Donde las dan las toman* for these interesting letters inserted in the text.

25. Iriarte, *Obras*, VI, 278–79.

26. *Ibid.*, p. 292.

27. *Ibid.*, I, 141.

28. *Ibid.*, p. 151.

29. *Ibid.*, p. 199.

30. *Ibid.*, p. xxxi.

31. *Ibid.*, pp. 159–60.

Chapter Three

1. Vézinet, *Molière, Florian Et La Littérature Espagnole*, p. 245.

2. Iriarte, *Obras*, I, 1–2.

3. Cotarelo, *Iriarte y su época*, p. 254.

4. Francisco Fernández González, *Historia de la crítica literaria en España desde Luzán hasta nuestros días* (Madrid: Imprenta de D. Alejandro Gómez Fuentenebro, 1867), p. 43.

5. Iriarte, *Literary Fables of Yriarte*, trans. George H. Devereux (Boston: Ticknor and Fields, 1855), pp. 44–45.

6. *Ibid.*, pp. 83–84.

7. *Ibid.*, pp. 99–100.

8. *Ibid.*, pp. 55–56.

9. *Ibid.*, pp. 79–81.

10. See Cotarelo, *Iriarte y su época*, p. 257, and the Clásicos Castel-

Notes and References

lanos edition of Iriarte's *Poesías,* ed. Alberto Navarro González (Madrid: Espasa-Calpe, 1953), pp. 92–93.

11. Iriarte, ed. Alberto Navarro González, pp. 94–96.
12. Iriarte, ed. Devereux, pp. 1–4.
13. Iriarte, *Obras,* VI, 377–78.
14. *Ibid.,* pp. 360–61.
15. *Ibid.,* pp. 362–63 and 367–68.
16. *Ibid.,* pp. 396–97.
17. Iriarte, ed. Devereux, p. 110.
18. *Ibid.,* p. 117.
19. *Ibid.,* p. 59.
20. *Ibid.,* p. 14.
21. *Ibid.,* p. 119.
22. *Ibid.,* p. 11.
23. Iriarte, *Obras,* VI, 383.
24. Iriarte, ed. Devereux, p. 107.
25. *Ibid.,* p. 9.
26. *Ibid.,* pp. 85–86.
27. *Ibid.,* p. 95.
28. *Ibid.,* p. 125.
29. *Ibid.,* pp. 136–38.
30. *Ibid.,* p. 7.
31. *Ibid.,* p. 19.
32. *Ibid.,* p. 34.
33. *Ibid.,* p. 65.
34. *Ibid.,* p. 71.
35. *Ibid.,* p. 69.
36. *Ibid.,* p. 61.
37. *Ibid.,* p. 122.
38. *Ibid.,* p. 145.
39. For a more complete bibliography of these translations and of all of Iriarte's work see: Agustín Millares Carlo, *Ensayo de una bio-bibliografía de escritores naturales de las Islas Canarias (siglos XVI, XVII y XVIII)* (Madrid: Tipografía de Archivos, 1932), pp. 258–318.

Chapter Four

1. A new edition of *El señorito mimado* and *La señorita mal-criada* from Editorial Castalia by Professor Russell Sebold is expected soon.
2. Charles E. Chapman's (*A History of Spain,* New York: Macmillan, 1918, pp. 420–21) concise description of the matter is pertinent here: "The simplicity and severity of Spanish customs were not maintained in matters of dress. There was a century-long conflict between the French and the native styles, the former represented by the military cut of clothing more in keeping with that of the present day,

and the latter by the slouched hat and long cape, as symbolic of the indigenous modes. On grounds of morality and public safety the government opposed the native type, which lent itself too easily to the facilitation of disguise, and the methodical Charles III even considered the imposition of a national dress which should omit the traditional features. A law of 1766 ordered their abandonment and the adoption of a short cape or riding coat and the three-cornered hat. The decree was the occasion of riots throughout Spain, and had to be recalled, while Squillace, the minister who had proposed it, lost his post. Aranda, his successor, achieved the desired end by indirect methods."

3. Iriarte, second of two unnumbered prefatory pages to *El filósofo casado* in *Obras*, V.

4. Leandro Fernández de Moratín, "Discurso preliminar," *Obras de Moratín* in *BAE*, 2 (Madrid: Imprenta de la Publicidad, 1850), 319.

5. Iriarte, *Obras*, IV, 130, 133.

6. *Ibid.*, p. 321.

7. *Ibid.*, p. 326.

8. Iriarte, *La señorita mal-criada, comedia moral en tres actos* (1788?), p. 22. (This publication is in a loose-leaf, printed form. It has no place of publication and the date has been pencilled in.)

9. *Ibid.*, p. 44.

10. Iriarte, *Obras*, V, 356.

11. Iriarte, *Colección de obras en verso y prosa* (Madrid: Imprenta Real, 1805), pp. 339–40.

12. José Subirá, *El compositor Iriarte (1751–1791) y el cultivo español del melólogo (melodrama)*, I (Barcelona: Consejo Superior de Investigaciones Científicas, 1949), 20.

13. *Ibid.*, p. 5.

Chapter Five

1. Forner, *Cotejo de las églogas* . . . , ed. Fernando Lázaro, pp. xviii–xix.

2. José Jurado, "Repercusiones del pleito con Iriarte en la obra de Forner," *Thesaurus*, 24, No. 2 (mayo-agosto, 1969), 228–77.

3. Forner, pp. 47–48.

4. Aguirre, pp. 217, 248.

5. Mariano José de Larra, "Literatura," *Artículos completos*, ed. Melchor de Almagro San Martín (Madrid: Aguilar, 1944), p. 748.

6. Manuel José Quintana, "Iriarte-Samaniego-Prosaísmo," in "Sobre la poesía castellana del siglo XVIII," *Obras completas* in *BAE*, 19 (Madrid: Imprenta y Estereotipía de M. Rivadeneyra, 1852), 151.

7. Marcelino Menéndez y Pelayo, *Horacio en España*, II (Madrid: Imprenta de A. Pérez Dubrull, 1885), 117–18.

8. Menéndez y Pelayo, *Historia de las ideas estéticas en España*,

Notes and References

III, ed. Enrique Sánchez Reyes (Santander: Aldus, S.A. de Artes Gráficas, 1940), 296–98.

9. Cotarelo, *Iriarte y su época*, p. 160.

10. *Ibid.*, pp. 150–52.

11. Alberto Navarro González, "Temas humanos en la poesía de Iriarte," *Revista de literatura*, I, No. 1 (enero-marzo, 1952), 7–8.

12. *Ibid.*, pp. 16–17.

13. *Ibid.*, p. 20.

14. *Ibid.*, pp. 23–24.

15. Russell P. Sebold, *Tomás de Iriarte: Poeta de "rapto racional"* ([Oviedo]: Universidad de Oviedo, 1961), p. 12.

16. *Ibid.*, pp. 17–18.

17. *Ibid.*, pp. 20–21.

18. *Ibid.*, p. 28.

19. *Ibid.*, p. 33.

20. *Ibid.*, p. 66.

Selected Bibliography

PRIMARY SOURCES

Works by Iriarte

Colección de obras en verso y prosa de Don Tomás de Yriarte. 6 vols. (Madrid: En la Imprenta de Benito Cano, 1787). First complete edition.

Colección de obras en verso y prosa de D. Tomás de Yriarte. 8 vols. (Madrid: En la Imprenta Real, 1805). Definitive edition.

La señorita mal-criada, comedia moral en tres actos (1788?). This publication is in a loose-leaf, printed form. It has no place of publication indicated and the date has been pencilled in. This particular copy is in the University of North Carolina library at Chapel Hill.

Poesías, ed. Alberto Navarro González (Madrid: Espasa-Calpe, 1953). An easily obtained edition but the introductory notes are of no extreme value.

Literary Fables of Yriarte, trans. George H. Devereux (Boston: Ticknor and Fields, 1855). A good English translation of interest as an example of American investigations concerning Iriarte.

(For more information the reader should consult Millares Carlo: see below.)

SECONDARY SOURCES

Book and Articles

AGUIRRE, ANTONIO. "La Notice De Carlos Pignatelli Sur Thomas De Yriarte," *Revue Hispanique*, 36 (1916), 200–252. Pignatelli's essay provides many intimate details not found elsewhere.

CHAPMAN, CHARLES E. *A History of Spain* (New York: Macmillan, 1918).

COOK, JOHN A. *Neo-Classic Drama in Spain. Theory and Practice* (Dallas: Southern Methodist University Press, 1959). An excellent study of the Neoclassic theater in Spain; a chapter is devoted to Iriarte.

COTARELO Y MORI, EMILIO. *Iriarte y su época* (Madrid: Est. Tipográfico "Sucesores de Rivadeneyra," 1897). One of the earliest, most important studies of Iriarte; a monumental work.

CUETO, LEOPOLDO AUGUSTO DE. "Bosquejo histórico-crítico de la poesía castellana en el siglo XVIII," *Poetas líricos del siglo XVIII,* I in *BAE,* 61 (Madrid: Imprenta de los Sucesores de Hernando, 1921). An early, comprehensive study of the Spanish eighteenth century.

FERNÁNDEZ GONZÁLEZ, FRANCISCO. *Historia de la crítica literaria en España desde Luzán hasta nuestros días* (Madrid: Imprenta de D. Alejandro Gómez Fuentenebro, 1867). Another early study presenting a wealth of details about this period.

FORNER, JUAN PABLO. *Cotejo de las églogas que ha premiado la Real Academia de la Lengua,* ed. Fernando Lázaro (Salamanca: Consejo Superior de Investigaciones Científicas, 1951). Lázaro's introduction is valuable for its generally unbiased discussion of Forner and Iriarte.

————. *Los gramáticos, historia chinesca,* ed. John H. R. Polt (Madrid: Editorial Castalia, 1970; Berkeley and Los Angeles: University of California Press, 1970). Polt's presentation of Forner is quite fair in its judgments. Excellent documentation.

————. *Los gramáticos, historia chinesca,* ed. José Jurado (Madrid: Espasa-Calpe, 1970). It's curious that two editions of this previously unedited work should appear in the same year. From the standpoint of sound scholarship and accurate documentation, Polt's edition is much to be preferred over this one.

FOULCHÉ-DELBOSC, RAYMOND. "Poesías inéditas de don Tomás de Yriarte," *Revue Hispanique,* 2 (1895), 70–76. These hitherto unpublished poems should be consulted with the appendix material in Cotarelo's volume.

HAMILTON, MARY NEAL. *Music in Eighteenth-Century Spain.* Illinois Studies in Language and Literature, No. 22 (Urbana: University of Illinois Press, 1937). A good companion to Subirá's study although it is more general in presentation.

JURADO, JOSÉ. "Repercusiones del pleito con Iriarte en la obra literaria de Forner," *Thesaurus,* 24, No. 2 (mayo-agosto, 1969), 228–77. Too long but a good article on the facts of the polemic between Forner and Iriarte that began in 1781.

LLORENTE, JUAN ANTONIO. *The History of the Inquisition of Spain from the Time of Its Establishment to the Reign of Ferdinand VII* (Translator not named) (London: Printed for Geo. B. Whittaker, 1826). A fascinating history of this Spanish institution with many salient points about various sixteenth-, seventeenth-, and eighteenth-century figures.

Selected Bibliography

McCLELLAND, I. L. *Spanish Drama of Pathos. 1750–1808*. 2 vols.
(Liverpool: Liverpool University Press, 1970). A valuable new
study of Spanish eighteenth-century drama with many specific
references to Iriarte.

MENÉNDEZ Y PELAYO, MARCELINO. *Historia de los heterodoxos espa-
ñoles*, V, ed. Enrique Sánchez Reyes. 8 vols. (Vols. 35–42 of the
Edición Nacional de las Obras Completas de Menéndez Pelayo)
(Santander: Aldus, S.A. de Artes Gráficas, 1947). See our Chapter
One.

————. *Historia de las ideas estéticas en España*, III, ed. Enrique
Sánchez Reyes. 5 vols. (Vols. 1–5 of the Edición Nacional de las
Obras Completas de Menéndez Pelayo) (Santander: Aldus, S.A.
de Artes Gráficas, 1940). See our Chapter Five.

————. *Horacio en España*, II. 2 vols. (Vols. 27 and 33 of Colección
de escritores castellanos) (Madrid: Imprenta de A. Pérez Dubrull,
1885). See our Chapter Five.

MILLARES CARLO, AGUSTÍN. *Ensayo de una bio-bibliografía de escritores naturales de las Islas Canarias (siglos XVI, XVII, XVIII)*,
Madrid: Tipografía de Archivos, 1932. An imposing and helpful
listing of Iriarte's works (pp. 258–318).

NAVARRO GONZÁLEZ, ALBERTO. "'Temas humanos en la poesía de
Iriarte," *Revista de literatura*, 1, No. 1 (enero-marzo, 1952), 7–24.
See our Chapter Five.

PELLISSIER, ROBERT E. *The Neo-Classic Movement in Spain During
the XVIII Century*. Leland Stanford Junior University Publications University Series, No. 30 (California: Stanford University
Press, 1918). A well-written, brief study that is a good companion
to Cook's investigations.

QUINTANA, MANUEL JOSÉ. "Iriarte-Samaniego-Prosaísmo" in "Sobre la
poesía castellana del siglo XVIII," *Obras completas* in BAE, 19
(Madrid: Imprenta y Estereotipía de M. Rivadeneyra, 1852).
See our Chapter Five.

RUBIO, ANTONIO. *La crítica del galicismo en España (1726–1832)*
(Mexico: La Universidad Nacional de México, 1937). An excellent synoptic view of the pro- and anti-French sentiments of
major writers of this period.

SARRAILH, JEAN. *L'Espagne Éclairée De La Seconde Moitié Du
XVIII Siècle* (Paris: Imprimerie Nationale, 1954). A very good
cultural, sociological, political study of the period.

SEBOLD, RUSSELL P. *Tomás de Iriarte: Poeta de "rapto racional"*
([Oviedo]: Universidad de Oviedo, 1961). See our Chapter Five.

SEMPERE Y GUARINOS, JUAN. *Ensayo de una biblioteca de los mejores
escritores del reynado de Carlos III*. 6 vols in 5 (Madrid: Imprenta Real, 1785–1789). Brief accounts of these writers and

their works. Excellent as a contemporary commentary. There is a fascimile reprint of this work made in 1963 in 3 vols. by the Dolphin Book Co.

SUBIRÁ, JOSÉ. *El compositor Iriarte (1750–1791) y el cultivo del meló-logo (melodrama)*. 2 vols. (Barcelona: Consejo Superior de Investigaciones Científicas, 1949–1950). A fascinating investigation of a little known genre; contains résumés of *melólogos*.

VÉZINET, FRANÇOIS. *Molière, Florian Et La Littérature Espagnole* (Paris: Librairie Hachette Et Cie., 1909). A small but interesting volume on mutual influences of certain French and Spanish writers. The author's tone is at times unnecessarily condescending, however.

VIERA Y CLAVIJO, JOSÉ DE. *Noticias de la historia general de las Islas Canarias,* Publicada con introducción, notas, índices e illustraciones a cargo de una junta editora bajo la dirección del Dr. Elías Serra Ràfols. 3 vols. (Santa Cruz de Tenerife: Goya-Ediciones, 1952). This work originally appeared in 1783. Besides being an intriguing study of contemporaries, the material on Iriarte presents many facts about him for the first time.

Index

[157]

Index

(El) mercurio histórico y político, 13, 22
Metastasio, Pietro, 32, 33, 76
Millares Carlo, Agustín, 149, 155
Miscellaneous Reflections, see Reflexiones sueltas
Moderns, 95, 98–100
Molière (Jean-Baptiste Poquelin), 79, 156
Moratín, Leandro Fernández de, 29, 38, 106, 115, 123, 124, 150
Moratín, Nicolás Fernández de, 12, 21, 106, 112, 128, 133, 135
Morell, Joseph, 63, 64, 65
motín de Esquilache, 107, 149–50
Music, see (La) música
(La) música, 13, 23, 32, 33, 38, 44, 61, 74–77, 127, 133, 134, 143

Navarrete, Eustaquio Fernández de, 45, 146
Navarrete, Martín Fernández de, see Fernández de Navarrete, Martín
Navarro González, Alberto, 138–40, 149, 151, 155
Neoclassicists, 12, 21, 111, 113, 114, 124, 125, 128, 142
(The) New Robinson, see (El) Nuevo Robinson
Nifo, Francisco Mariano, 107
Noticias de cuándo se inventaron las artes, 48
(El) nuevo Robinson, 14, 58

Obras poéticas de don Thomás de Iriarte, entresacadas de algunos de sus manuscritos, 40
Observaciones sobre las Fábulas literarias originales de D. Tomás de Iriarte, 14, 44
Official Translator of the First Secretariat of State, 12, 15, 22, 24
Olavide, Pablo de, 28, 29, 48
Oración apologética por la España, 51
Order of Charles III, 12, 22
Oropesa, Bárbara de las Nieves de (mother of Iriarte), 12, 18
Osuna, Duchess of, 35, 58, 59

Paleografía griega, 16
(The) Pampered Youth, see (El) señorito mimado
Para casos tales suelen tener los maestros oficiales, 13, 42, 44, 47, 88-95, 97, 130
Parnaso español, 13, 27, 28, 64, 73, 82, 83
Pellicer, Juan Antonio, 32
Pellissier, Robert E., 155
Phaedrus, 40
Philip V, king of Spain, 29
Pignatelli, Carlos, 25, 28, 32, 33, 40, 59, 60, 132, 133, 145, 147, 154
Plan de una Academia de Ciencias y Bellas Artes, 13, 34, 35
Plan For an Academy of Sciences and Letters, see Plan de una Academia de Ciencias y Bellas Artes
(La) poética, trans. of, 13, 26, 27, 44, 46, 61–73, 78, 93, 124, 143
Poetics, see (La) poética
Polt, John H. R., 154
Profecía política, 25
Puerto de la Cruz, 12, 15, 19
Pygmalion, 127

Quintana, Manuel José, 134, 141, 150, 155

Ramos, Enrique, 29, 145
Reflections Concerning the Eclogue Batilo, see Reflexiones sobre la égloga de Batilo
Reflexiones sobre la égloga de Batilo, 13, 30, 31, 130
Reflexiones sueltas, 13, 34, 35
Rioja, Francisco de, 133
Ríos, Vicente de los, 27, 28, 72, 82, 148
Rojo, Juan Bernardino, 49
Ronquido, 25
Rousseau, Jean-Jacques, 127
Rubio, Antonio, 155

sainetes, 20, 125
Samaniego, Félix María de, 14, 42, 43, 44, 45, 49, 53, 54, 59, 80, 88, 133, 144, 146, 155

Index